BIRDS *of* CHICAGO

Including NE Illinois & NW Indiana

Chris C. Fisher
David B. Johnson

LONE
PINE

The Publisher: Lone Pine Publishing

1901 Raymond Ave. SW, Suite C	206, 10426 – 81 Ave.	202A, 1110 Seymour St.
Renton, WA 98055	Edmonton, AB T6E 1X5	Vancouver, BC V6B 3N3
USA	Canada	Canada

Website: http://www.lonepinepublishing.com

Canadian Cataloguing in Publication Data

Fisher, Chris C. (Christopher Charles)
    Birds of Chicago

        Includes bibliographical references and index.
        ISBN 1-55105-112-5

        1. Birds—Illinois—Chicago—Identification. 2. Bird watching—Illinois—Chicago. I. Johnson, David B. (David Bruce), 1951–
II. Title.
QL684.I3F57 1998   598'.09773'11   C97-910647-8

Senior Editor: Nancy Foulds
Project Editor: Roland Lines
Production Manager: David Dodge
Layout and Production: Michelle Bynoe
Cover Illustration: Gary Ross
Cartography: Volker Bodegom
Illustrations: Gary Ross, Ted Nordhagen, Ewa Pluciennik
Separations and Film: Elite Lithographers Co., Edmonton, Alberta
Printing: Quality Colour Press, Edmonton, Alberta

The checklist of Chicago-area birds (pp. 152–55) is reprinted from *Birds of the Greater Chicago Area: A Seasonal Checklist* with the kind permission of the Chicago Audubon Society. © 1982 Chicago Audubon Society, revised 1998.

The publisher gratefully acknowledges the assistance of the Department of Canadian Heritage.

Contents

Acknowledgments

A book such as this is made possible by the inspired work of Chicago's naturalist community and birding societies—the Chicago Audubon Society, Chicago Ornithological Society, Illinois Audubon Society, Illinois Ornithological Society and Evanston North Shore Bird Club, among others—which all make daily contributions to natural history, and whose contributions continue to advance the science of ornithology and to motivate a new generation of nature lovers.

My thanks go to Gary Ross and Ted Nordhagen, whose illustrations have elevated the quality of this book; to Carole Patterson, for her continual support; to the team at Lone Pine Publishing—Roland Lines, Nancy Foulds, Eloise Pulos, Michelle Bynoe and Shane Kennedy—for their input and steering; to John Acorn and Jim Butler, for their stewardship and their remarkable passion; and to Wayne Campbell, a premier naturalist whose works have served as models of excellence.

Chris C. Fisher

My thanks go to my mother, Jaynell, who encouraged me to be a summer camp naturalist for the Boy Scouts of America and who sent me my first bird tapes at camp (these I still have!); to Dad, Wib, who taught me my first bird call and who went on so many great birding adventures with me; and to my family, Jeri, Evan and Daren, who so graciously endure my birding obsessions. A special thanks must go to Larry Balch, who recommended that I take on this project; to Laurie Binford, Richard Biss, Lynne Carpenter, Charles T. Clark, Steven Mlodinow, James Neal, Joel Greenberg, Andy Sigler, Robert Hughes, Gerald Rosenband, Penny and Tom Pucelik, and Patti and Jim Ware, all of whom influenced my passion for birding. I must thank my late father-in-law, Dr. Samuel Pollack, who saw 'birds burnt into my retinas' and said someday I'd be involved in writing a bird book. He was right! Finally, I must thank the team of Lone Pine Publishing editors, publishers, proofreaders, writers and naturalists who suffered through my idiosyncracies.

David B. Johnson

Introduction

No matter where we live, birds are a natural part of our lives. We are so used to seeing them that we often take their presence for granted. When we take the time to notice their colors, songs and behaviors, we experience their dynamic appeal.

This book presents a brief introduction into the lives of birds. It is intended to serve as both a bird identification guide and a bird appreciation guide. Getting to know the names of birds is the first step toward getting to know birds. Once we've made contact with a species, we can better appreciate its character and mannerisms during future encounters. Over a lifetime of meetings, many birds become acquaintances, some seen daily, others not for years.

It would be impossible for a beginners' book such as this to comprehensively describe all the birds of the Chicago region. The selection of species within this book represents a balance between the familiar and the noteworthy. Many of the 126 species described in this guide are the most common species found in the Chicago area; others are less common, but they are noteworthy because they are important ecologically or because their particular status grants them a high profile. There is no one site where all the species in this book can be observed simultaneously, but most species can be viewed—at least seasonally—within a short drive from Chicago.

It is hoped that this guide will inspire novice birdwatchers into spending some time outdoors, gaining valuable experience with the local bird community. This book stresses the identity of birds, but it also attempts to bring them to life by discussing their various character traits. We often discuss a bird's character traits in human terms, because personifying a bird's character can help us to feel a bond with the birds. The perceived links with birds should not be mistaken for actual behaviors, as our interpretations can falsely reflect the complexities of bird life.

FEATURES OF THE LANDSCAPE

The variety of habitats around Chicago are home to a rich diversity of birds: more than 300 of our state's regularly occurring bird species have been found in and around our area. Situated along Lake Michigan and the Chicago River system, the Chicago area is a favorite spot for a wide variety of bird life.

The lakeshores and river valleys around Chicago act as natural pathways, funneling birds along their north-south migration routes. Stretches of beach and rocky shores strewn with pockets of shrubs and deciduous forests provide habitat and foraging opportunities for many birds. Along these shorelines, thousands of migrating geese, ducks, shorebirds, gulls and other birds stop to replenish their energy supplies, moving from one productive foraging site to another. Areas around Chicago's lakefront, such as Montrose Beach and Waukegan Harbor, are great for viewing waterfowl and other migrating birds in spring and fall. These waters remain open during winter, and many ducks and gulls can still be seen in our area.

Some of the most productive bird habitats are the inland lakes, sloughs and marsh areas common around the Chicago region. An abundance of plant and animal life attracts many migrating species, and during the breeding season, many birds build their nests along lakeshores or among the tall grasses and cattails of marshland edges. A visit to the McGinnis Slough or the lakes and marshes at Lake Calumet will inevitably offer rewarding birding opportunities: geese, grebes and ducks are common in these habitats, and during summer these wetlands are favored breeding spots for herons, egrets and coots.

Although most original prairie and grassland has disappeared from Illinois—the destruction of valuable habitat continues to be a significant factor contributing to a loss of bird life in our state—many prairie birds have adapted well to a new environment of pastures, woodland edges and roadside thickets. The hedgerows, edge habitats and uncultivated, grassy fields of the countryside provide shelter for a variety of migrant and nesting species. During spring and summer, look for sparrows, larks and blackbirds foraging for seeds and insects along open fields and roadsides. The fields and grassland areas of Illinois Beach State Park in Lake County offer unique year-round opportunities for the avid birder: during summer, these habitats provide nesting sites for many birds; in fall, great numbers of hawks can be seen passing overhead on their way south.

Broadleaf forests, including pockets of trees in backyards and city parks, are where you will find many of our songbirds. Every spring and fall, incredible numbers of woodland migrants funnel through our area, inundating local forest communities with exciting chatter and colorful song. At this time of year, areas such as Lincoln Park and the Swallow Cliff Forest Preserve become

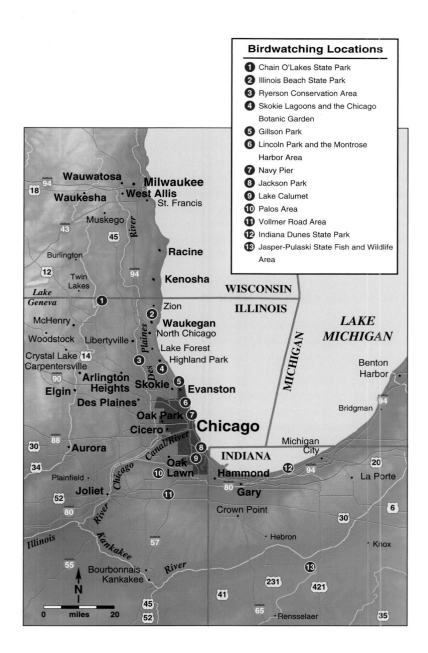

Birdwatching Locations

1. Chain O'Lakes State Park
2. Illinois Beach State Park
3. Ryerson Conservation Area
4. Skokie Lagoons and the Chicago Botanic Garden
5. Gillson Park
6. Lincoln Park and the Montrose Harbor Area
7. Navy Pier
8. Jackson Park
9. Lake Calumet
10. Palos Area
11. Vollmer Road Area
12. Indiana Dunes State Park
13. Jasper-Pulaski State Fish and Wildlife Area

a bustling of activity as flycatchers, thrushes, vireos, warblers, sparrows and orioles take refuge in mixed stands of oak, maple, spruce and pine. Many warblers have endured exhausting flights on their migratory travels, and local woodlands provide much welcomed food, water and shelter. Wooded areas commonly found along streams, creeks and ponds are also favored habitat. A variety of species, including the Wood Duck, Warbling Vireo and Louisiana Waterthrush, rely on riparian habitats for feeding and sometimes for nest building.

The landscaped setting and rural neighborhoods of our city are also good places to become acquainted with bird life. Backyard feeders are a welcome invitation for many species during the colder months, and to the delight of area residents, many birds make use of nest boxes in summer. City parks and backyards are permanent homes for a long list of birds, including the Blue Jay, Cedar Waxwing, Northern Cardinal, American Goldfinch and a variety of woodpeckers. Urban development has also created new habitat for birds such as the Rock Dove, House Wren, European Starling and House Sparrow, which are exceptionally adapted to these settings and thrive in our human-made environment.

THE IMPORTANCE OF HABITAT

Understanding the relationships between habitats and bird species often helps identify which birds are which. Because you won't find a loon up a tree or a pheasant on a lake, habitat is an important thing to note when birdwatching.

The quality of habitat is one of the most powerful factors to influence bird distribution, and with experience you might become amazed by the predictability of some birds within a specific habitat type. The habitat icons in this book show where each species is most likely to be seen. It is important to realize, however, that because of their migratory habits, birds sometimes turn up in completely different habitats. These unexpected surprises, despite being confusing to novice birders, are among the most powerful motivations for the increasing legion of birdwatchers.

Lakes and
Open water

Shorelines

Marshes
and Wetlands

Parks and
Gardens

Fields and
Shrubby Areas

Coniferous
Forests

Broadleaf
Forests

THE ORGANIZATION OF THIS BOOK

To simplify field identification, *Birds of Chicago* is organized slightly differently from other field guides, many of which use strict phylogenetic groupings. In cases where many birds from the same family are described, conventional groupings are maintained in this book. In other cases, however, distantly related birds that share physical and behavioral similarities are grouped together. This blend of family groupings and groups of physically similar species strives to help the novice birdwatcher identify and appreciate the birds he or she encounters.

DIVING BIRDS

loons, grebes, cormorants

These heavy-bodied birds are adapted to diving for their food. Between their underwater foraging dives, they are most frequently seen on the surface of the water. These birds could only be confused with one another or with certain diving ducks.

WETLAND WADERS

herons, cranes, rails, coots

Although members of this group vary considerably in size and represent three separate families of birds, wetland waders share similar habitat and food preferences. Some of these long-legged birds are quite common in marshes, but certain species are heard far more than they are seen.

WATERFOWL

geese, ducks

Waterfowl tend to have stout bodies and webbed feet, and they are swift in flight. Although most species are associated with water, waterfowl can sometimes be seen grazing on upland sites.

VULTURES, HAWKS AND FALCONS

From deep forests to open country to large lakes, there are hawks and falcons hunting the skies. Their predatory look—sharp talons, hooked bills and forward-facing eyes—easily identifies members of this group. They generally forage during the day, and hawks and vultures use their broad wings to soar in thermals and updrafts.

PHEASANTS

These introduced Asian gamebirds bear a superficial resemblance to chickens. They are long, sleek birds and poor flyers, and they are most often encountered on the ground or when flushed.

SHOREBIRDS

plovers, sandpipers, woodcocks, etc.

Although these small, generally long-legged, swift-flying birds are mainly found along shores, don't be surprised to find some species in pastures and marshy areas.

GULLS AND TERNS

Gulls are relatively large, usually light-colored birds that are frequently seen swimming, walking about in urban areas or soaring gracefully over the city. Their backs tend to be darker than their bellies, and their feet are webbed. Terns are in the same family as gulls, but they rarely soar and they have straight, pointed bills.

DOVES AND PARROTS

Both of our doves are easily recognizable. Rock Doves are found in all urban areas, from city parks to the downtown core, but they have many of the same physical and behavioral characteristics as the 'wilder' Mourning Doves. The Monk Parakeet was introduced to Chicago from the jungles of South America.

NOCTURNAL BIRDS

owls, nightjars

These night hunters all have large eyes. Owls, which primarily prey on rodents, have powerful, taloned feet and strongly hooked bills. Nightjars, which catch moths and other nocturnal insects on the wing, have extremely large mouths.

KINGFISHERS

The Belted Kingfisher's behavior and physical characteristics are quite unlike any other bird's in Chicago. It primarily hunts fish, plunging after them from the air or from an overhanging perch.

WOODPECKERS

The drumming sound as they hammer wood and their precarious foraging habits easily identify most woodpeckers. They are frequently seen in forests, clinging to trunks and chipping away bark with their straight, sturdy bills. Even when these birds can't be seen or heard, you can find their characteristic marks on trees in any mature forest.

HUMMINGBIRDS

The Ruby-throated Hummingbird is Chicago's smallest bird. Its bright colors and swift flight are very characteristic.

FLYCATCHERS

wood-pewees, flycatchers, kingbirds

These birds might be best identified by their foraging behavior. As the name implies, flycatchers catch insects on the wing, darting after them from a favorite perch. Many flycatchers have subdued plumage, but kingbirds are rather boldly marked.

SWIFTS AND SWALLOWS

Members of these two families are typically seen at their nest sites or in flight. Small and sleek, swallows fly gracefully in pursuit of insects. Swifts are small, dark birds with long, narrow wings and short tails, and they have a more 'mechanical' flight behavior.

JAYS AND CROWS

Many members of this family are known for their intelligence and adaptability. These birds are easily observed, and they are often extremely bold, teasing the animal-human barrier. They are sometimes called 'corvids,' from Corvidae, the scientific name for the family.

SMALL SONGBIRDS

chickadees, wrens, kinglets, etc.

Birds in this group are all generally smaller than a sparrow. Many of them associate with one another in mixed-species flocks, and they are commonly encountered in city parks, backyards and other wooded areas.

BLUEBIRDS AND THRUSHES

bluebirds, thrushes, robins

From the bold robin to the secretive forest thrushes, this group of beautiful singers has the finest collective voice. Although some thrushes are very familiar, others require a little experience and patience to identify.

VIREOS AND WARBLERS

Vireos tend to dress in pale olive, whereas warblers are splashed liberally with colors. All these birds are very small, and they sing characteristic courtship songs, typically in woods and thickets.

MID-SIZED SONGBIRDS

tanagers, starlings, thrashers, etc.

The birds within this group are all sized between a sparrow and a robin. Tanagers are very colorful and sing complex, flute-like songs, but waxwings are more reserved in dress and voice. Starlings are frequently seen and heard all over the Chicago area.

SPARROWS

towhees, sparrows, juncos

These small, often indistinct birds are predominantly brown and streaky, and their songs are often very useful in identification. Many birdwatchers discount sparrows as 'little brown birds'—towhees are colorful exceptions—but they are worthy of the extra identification effort.

BLACKBIRDS AND ORIOLES

blackbirds, meadowlarks, cowbirds, etc.

Most of these birds are predominantly black and have relatively long tails. They are common in open areas, city parks and agricultural fields. The Eastern Meadowlark is also part of this family, despite not being black and having a short tail.

FINCH-LIKE BIRDS

finches, cardinals, grosbeaks, etc.

These finches and finch-like birds are primarily adapted to feeding on seeds, and they have stout, conical bills. Many are bird-feeder regulars, and they are a familiar part of the winter scene.

MEASUREMENTS

The size measurement given for each bird is an average length of the bird from the tip of its bill to the tip of its tail. It is an approximate measurement of the bird as it is seen in nature (rather than a measurement of stuffed specimens, which tend to be straighter and therefore longer).

In many situations, it is more useful to know a bird's comparative size, rather than its actual length in inches, so the 'Quick I.D.' for each species describes the bird's size in relation to a common, well-known bird (for example, sparrow-sized, smaller than a robin, etc.). It must be remembered that these are general impressions of size that are influenced as much by the bulk of a bird as by its total length.

PLUMAGES

One of the complications to birdwatching is that many species look different in spring and summer than they do in fall and winter—they have what are generally called *breeding* and *non-breeding* plumages—and young birds often look quite different from their parents. This book does not try to describe or illustrate all the different plumages of a species; instead, it focuses on the forms that are most commonly seen and are the easiest to identify in our area. All the illustrations are of adult birds.

ABUNDANCE CHARTS

Accompanying each bird description is a chart that indicates the relative abundance of the species throughout the year. These stylized graphs offer some insight

into the distribution and abundance of the birds, but they should not be viewed as definitive—they represent a generalized overview. There could be inconsistencies specific to time and location, but these charts should provide readers with a basic reference for bird abundance and occurrence.

Each chart is divided into the 12 months of the year. The pale orange that colors the chart is an indication of abundance: the higher the color, the more common the bird. Dark orange is used to indicate the nesting period. The time frame is approximate, however, and nesting birds can sometimes be found both before and after the period indicated on the chart. If no nesting color is shown, the bird breeds outside the Chicago area, or it visits Chicago in significant numbers only during migration or winter.

These graphs are based on personal observations and on local references, including those listed on p. 151.

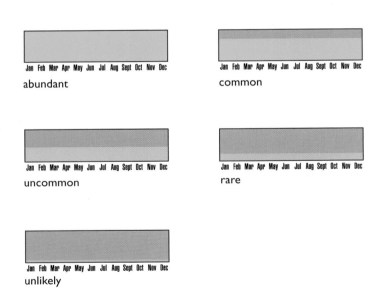

abundant

common

uncommon

rare

unlikely

BIRDS
of CHICAGO
Including NE Illinois & NW Indiana

Common Loon
Gavia immer

The Common Loon is a symbol of northern wilderness, preferring the diminishing pristine areas where birds alone quarrel over boreal wetlands. They do not breed in our area, but visit Chicago each year during migration. Listen for their primeval wilderness voice during spring, when passing birds practice their courting songs. Their intricate, almost reptilian, dark green–and–white breeding plumage can be seen in spring among the 80-plus glacial lakes in Lake County or off Lake Michigan's shoreline as the birds wait for the ice to melt on interior lakes. In fall, loons can best be seen migrating offshore or floating in the waters off Illinois Beach State Park and Navy Pier.

Loons routinely poke their heads underwater, spotting potential prey and plotting their forthcoming pursuit. They dive deeply and efficiently, compressing their feathers to reduce underwater drag and to decrease their buoyancy. Propelling themselves primarily with their legs, these birds can outswim some fish over short distances. Because they have solid bones (unlike most other birds) and because their legs are placed well back on their bodies for diving, Common Loons require long stretches of open water for take-off.

Similar Species: Common Merganser (p. 40) has a red bill and very white plumage. Double-crested Cormorant (p. 20) has all-black plumage, a long neck and an orange bill, and it usually holds its head pointed upward when it swims. Red-throated Loon is smaller and has a slimmer bill and a rounded head.

breeding

Quick I.D.: larger than a duck; sexes similar; stout, long, dagger-like bill. *Breeding:* dark green-black hood; black-and-white checkerboard back; fine, black-and-white 'necklace.' *Non-breeding:* sandy-brown back; whitish underparts. *In flight:* hunchbacked.
Size: 27–33 in.

Jan Feb Mar Apr May Jun Jul Aug Sept Oct Nov Dec

Pied-billed Grebe
Podilymbus podiceps

The small, stout, drab body of the Pied-billed Grebe seems perfectly suited to its marshy habitat, but its loud, whooping *kuk-kuk-cow-cow-cow-cowp-cowp* is a sound that seems more at home in tropical rainforests. Pied-billed Grebes can be found on most freshwater wetlands that are surrounded by cattails, bulrushes or other emergent vegetation. These diving birds are frustrating to follow as they disappear and then reappear, with only their heads appearing above the water's surface.

During summer, these small, reclusive grebes often nest within view of lakeside trails. They build nests that float on the water's surface, and their eggs often rest in waterlogged vegetation. Young grebes take their first swim soon after hatching, but they will instinctively clamber aboard a parent's back at the first sign of danger.

Similar Species: Ducks have bills that are flattened top to bottom. Horned Grebe and Eared Grebe have light underparts.

breeding

Jan Feb Mar Apr May Jun Jul Aug Sept Oct Nov Dec

Quick I.D.: smaller than a duck; sexes similar; all brown. *Breeding:* dark vertical band on thick, pale, blue-gray bill; black chin. *First-year* (summer/fall): striped brown and white. **Size:** 12–14 in.

Double-crested Cormorant
Phalacrocorax auritus

When Double-crested Cormorants fly in single-file, low over Lake Michigan, the prehistoric sight hints to their ancestry. The tight, dark flocks soar over lakes, until hunger or the need for rest draws them to the water's surface. It is there that cormorants are most comfortable, disappearing beneath the surface in deep foraging dives or resting atop the water.

Cormorants lack the ability to waterproof their feathers, so they need to dry their wings after each swim. These large, black waterbirds are frequently seen perched on dead trees, piers or jetties, with their wings partially spread to expose their wet feathers to the sun and the wind. It would seem to be a great disadvantage for a waterbird to have to dry its wings, but the cormorant's ability to wet its feathers decreases its buoyancy, making it easier for it to swim after the fish on which it preys. Sealed nostrils, a long, rudder-like tail and excellent underwater vision are other features of the Double-crested Cormorant's aquatic lifestyle.

Similar Species: Common Loon (p. 18) has a shorter neck and is more stout overall.

breeding

Quick I.D.: goose-sized; sexes similar; all black; long tail; long neck. *Breeding:* bright orange bill and throat pouch; black plumes streaming back from eyebrows (seen only at close range). *First-year:* brown; pale neck, breast and belly. *In flight:* kinked neck; rapid wingbeats.
Size: 30–35 in.

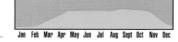

Jan Feb Mar Apr May Jun Jul Aug Sept Oct Nov Dec

Great Blue Heron
Ardea herodias

breeding

The Great Blue Heron is one of the largest and most noticed herons in our area. It often stands motionless as it surveys the calm waters, its graceful lines blending naturally with the grasses and cattails of wetlands. All herons have specialized vertebrae that enable the neck to fold back over itself. The S-shaped neck, seen in flight, identifies all members of this wading family.

Hunting herons space themselves out evenly in favorite hunting spots, and they will strike out suddenly at prey below the water's surface. In flight, their lazy wingbeats slowly but effortlessly carry them up to their nests. These herons nest communally, high in trees, building bulky stick nests that are sometimes in plain sight of urban areas. Almost any wetland produces good views of this bird, which is common in spring, summer and fall and uncommon in winter.

Similar Species: None.

Jan Feb Mar Apr May Jun Jul Aug Sept Oct Nov Dec

Quick I.D.: very large heron; eagle-sized wingspan; sexes similar; gray-blue plumage; red thighs; long, dagger-like, yellow bill. *In flight:* head folded back; legs held straight back.
Size: 48–52 in.

Green Heron
Butorides virescens

This crow-sized heron is far less conspicuous than its Great Blue cousin. The Green Heron prefers to hunt for frogs and small fish in shallow, weedy wetlands, where it is often seen perched just above the water's surface. By searching the shallow, shady, overgrown wetland edges around lakes, rivers and open marshes, Chicago's birders can get a prolonged view of this reclusive bird.

The Green Heron often uses all of its stature to hunt over a favorite site. With its bright yellow feet clasping a branch or reed, this small heron stretches nearly horizontally over the water, its pose rigid and unchanging, until a fish swims into range. Like a taut bowstring, the tension mounts until the heron chooses to fire. Lunging its entire body at the prey, it is often soaked to the shoulders following a successful hunt.

Similar Species: Black-crowned Night-Heron (p. 23) is larger and has light underparts. American Bittern is larger and heavily streaked, and lacks any green color.

Quick I.D.: crow-sized; sexes similar; small, stubby heron; short legs; glossy green back; chestnut nape and throat; dark cap. *Breeding male:* orange legs. *Immature:* less colorful, with more streaking in throat and breast.
Size: 18–21 in.

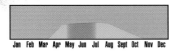

Jan Feb Mar Apr May Jun Jul Aug Sept Oct Nov Dec

Black-crowned Night-Heron
Nycticorax nycticorax

breeding

As daylight fades, a distinctive *wok-wok* call announces a flock of Black-crowned Night-Herons flying to a marsh to feed. These birds prefer to feed at this time of day, and their shapes can be among the last forms visible in summer's golden evening light. These white-plumed, pony-tailed birds possess remarkably large eyes, a possible advantage in their nocturnal foraging efforts.

Black-crowned Night-Herons are much more difficult to find in the middle of the day, because they roost inconspicuously in shoreline vegetation. They nest in low bushes, and have generally become increasingly uncommon in our area in the past decades. The degradation and destruction of vital wetlands have resulted in a sharp decline in this bird's abundance, and it has been included on the Illinois State Endangered Species List. The Black-crowned Night-Heron is one of the world's most abundant and widespread herons, so its endangered status in Illinois strongly signals the state's dire need for increased wetland conservation.

Similar Species: Great Blue Heron (p. 21) is larger and has a long neck. Green Heron (p. 22) has a greenish-black cap, a chestnut neck and greenish upperparts. American Bittern is similar to a juvenile night-heron, but it has black wing tips and a black mustache stripe. Yellow-crowned Night-Heron has a white cheek patch and crown.

Quick I.D.: mid-sized heron; sexes similar; black crown and back; gray neck and wings; white cheek and belly; moderately long legs. *Breeding:* white plumes from back of head. *Juvenile:* brown; heavily streaked and spotted. **Size:** 24–26 in.

Jan Feb Mar Apr May Jun Jul Aug Sept Oct Nov Dec

Sandhill Crane
Grus canadensis

The Sandhill Crane's deep, rolling, guttural rattle announces the presence of a migrating flock long before the birds can be seen on the horizon. The loud chorus—*ga-rooo ga-rooo!*—precedes the high-flying birds and alerts attentive naturalists to one of Illinois's most marvelous spectacles. During migration, Sandhill Cranes pass over the Jasper-Pulaski State Fish and Wildlife Area by the thousands.

Sandhill Cranes are among the largest of the birds that can be seen in our area. They stand as high as a pre-teenage child, they have a wingspan the height of a professional basketball player, and they have a voice matched only by the most powerful of opera singers. Occasionally, during spring and fall, a flock might land on surrounding farmlands in our area. There they feast on waste grain and corn before continuing on their voyage. The sights and sounds of these great birds enable urban residents to connect vicariously to far-off wilderness areas.

Similar Species: Great Blue Heron (p. 21) flies with its neck arched over its shoulders and lacks the red forehead patch.

Quick I.D.: very large bird; sexes similar; pale gray plumage; long, slender neck; long, thin, dark legs; naked red crown; long, straight bill; plumage often stained rusty from iron oxides in water. *Juvenile:* no red patch; light plumage with patches of orange-red. *In flight:* neck fully extended; legs extended; slow downbeat; quick upstroke.
Size: 41–47 in.

Jan Feb Mar Apr May Jun Jul Aug Sept Oct Nov Dec

Sora
Porzana carolina

Skulking around freshwater marshes in the Chicago area is the seldom-seen Sora. Although this rail arrives in good numbers in spring, it is not a species that can be encountered with any predictability. Visual meetings with the Sora in Chicago arise unexpectedly, usually when birdwatchers are out in good wetlands searching for less reclusive species. At other times this bird unexpectedly shows up in a bush along the waterfront, such as in the Magic Hedge at the Montrose Promontory. Although it has declined in our area, its loud call, *So-ra, So-ra,* followed by a descending whinny, can still be heard at many area marshes.

Urban sprawl and agricultural expansion have come at the expense of many Chicago birds. The Sora's marshland habitat is often thought to be unproductive by human standards, but these shallow, nutrient-rich wetlands host a bounty of wildlife. With the growing legion of birdwatchers and nature lovers, societal values might finally shift toward an understanding of our natural communities and wetland protection.

Similar Species: Virginia Rail has a long, reddish, downcurved bill.

breeding

Jan Feb Mar Apr May Jun Jul Aug Sept Oct Nov Dec

Quick I.D.: robin-sized; sexes similar; short, yellow bill; front of face is black; gray neck and breast; long, greenish legs.
Size: 8–10 in.

American Coot
Fulica americana

The American Coot is a mix of comedy and confusion: it seems to have been made up of bits and pieces leftover from other birds. It has the lobed toes of a grebe, the bill of a chicken and the body shape and swimming habits of a duck, but it is not remotely related to any of these species: its closest cousins are rails and cranes. American Coots dabble and dive in water and forage on land, and they eat both plant and animal matter. They can be found in just about every freshwater pond, lake, marsh, lagoon or city park in Chicago, and during migration they can number in the thousands.

These loud, grouchy birds are seen chugging along in wetlands, frequently entering into short-lived disputes with other coots. American Coots appear comical while they swim: their heads bob in time with their paddling feet, and as a coot's swimming speed increases, so does the back-and-forth motion of its head. At peak speed, this motion seems to disorient the coot, so it prefers to run, flap and splash to the other side of the wetland.

Similar Species: All ducks and grebes generally lack the uniform black color and the white bill.

Quick I.D.: smaller than a duck; sexes similar; black body; white bill; red forehead shield; short tail; long legs; lobed feet; white undertail coverts.
Size: 14–16 in.

Jan Feb Mar Apr May Jun Jul Aug Sept Oct Nov Dec

Canada Goose
Branta canadensis

Most flocks of Canada Geese in city parks and golf courses show little concern for their human neighbors. These urban geese seem to think nothing of creating a traffic jam, blocking a fairway or dining on lawns and gardens. Their love of manicured parks and gardens and the lack of predators have created a population explosion in the Chicago area.

Breeding pairs of Canada Geese are regal in appearance and their loyalty is legendary—they mate for life, and it's common for a mate to stay at the side of a fallen partner. Canada Geese are common throughout the Chicago area during every season of the year.

Similar Species: None.

Jan Feb Mar Apr May Jun Jul Aug Sept Oct Nov Dec

Quick I.D.: large goose; sexes similar; white cheek; black head and neck; brown body; white undertail coverts.
Size: 35–42 in.

Wood Duck
Aix sponsa

Only days old, small Wood Duck ducklings are lured out of the only world they know by their pleading mother. Although this seems typical of most ducks, young Wood Ducks require more coaxing than most—their nest is an old woodpecker hole high in a tree. With a faith-filled leap, the cottonball ducklings tumble toward the ground, often bouncing on impact. When all the siblings have leapt into the waiting world, they follow their mother through the dense underbrush to the nearest water.

Many of the old, rotten, hollow lakeside trees that provided excellent nesting sites for Wood Ducks have diminished in the Chicago area. As a result, more and more young Wood Ducks are beginning life by tumbling out of nest boxes made by humans. The Wood Ducks are provided with a secure nest site in which to incubate their eggs, while landowners have the honor of having North America's most handsome ducks living on their land. The male Wood Duck is one of the continent's most colorful birds; no other duck can match his much-celebrated, iridescent, colorful and intricate plumage.

Similar Species: Male is very distinctive. Female resembles many other small, female ducks, but has a prominent, wide, white eye ring.

Quick I.D.: small duck. *Male:* glossy green head; crest slicked back from crown; white chin and throat; chestnut breast spotted white; white shoulder slash; golden sides; dark back and hindquarters. *Female:* white teardrop eye patch; mottled brown breast streaked white; brown-gray upperparts; white belly.
Size: 18–20 in.

Jan Feb Mar Apr May Jun Jul Aug Sept Oct Nov Dec

American Wigeon

Anas americana

During spring and fall migration, American Wigeons can easily be found and identified in the sloughs of Chicago's flooded fields and lakes. Flocks of wigeons waddle across lawns at Gillson Park or Waukegan Harbor, begging scraps intended for pigeons. The white top and gray sides of the male American Wigeon's head look somewhat like a balding scalp, while the nasal *wee-he-he-he* calls sound remarkably like the squeaks of a squeezed rubber ducky.

Although they breed to the north and winter primarily on the Atlantic, American Wigeons are becoming increasingly visible in our area during their passage. At this time of year hundreds can be seen in such areas as Lake Calumet, refueling for the continuation of their trip.

Similar Species: Green-winged Teal is smaller and has a white shoulder slash and a rusty head with a green swipe.

Quick I.D.: mid-sized duck; cinnamon breast and flanks; white belly; gray bill with black tip; green speculum. *Male:* white forehead; green swipe running back from eye. *Female:* no distinct color on head.

Size: 18–21 in.

Jan Feb Mar Apr May Jun Jul Aug Sept Oct Nov Dec

American Black Duck
Anas rubripes

Among the flocks of waterfowl wintering on open water in the Chicago area, you will find the plain-looking American Black Duck. Like a dark version of the familiar Mallard (except for its silver wing linings, dark orange feet and purple wing patch), the American Black Duck is the classic duck of eastern North America, traditionally having a stronghold throughout the Great Lakes states.

Unfortunately the eastern expansion of Mallards has come at the expense of this dark dabbler. As its green-headed cousin spread into our area, the American Black Duck quickly hybridized with the Mallard. This genetic watering down of pure American Black Duck stock has concerned biologists, and the future stability of this species is unknown. Habitat loss and the degradation of wetlands in general have further contributed to the decline of this bird. Although plain in appearance, the state of the American Black Duck's future increases its profile in the eyes and minds of conservation-oriented naturalists.

Similar Species: Mallard (p. 31) has an overall lighter body plumage and a blue speculum, and the male has a green head.

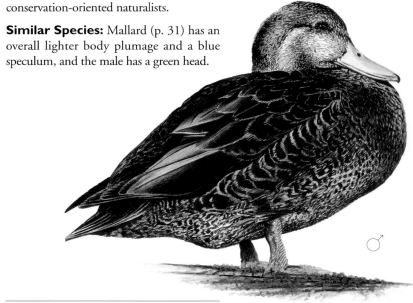

Quick I.D.: large duck; dark blackish-brown body; light brown head and neck; violet speculum; bright orange feet. *Male:* yellow bill. *Female:* dull green bill spotted with black. *In flight:* silver-lined wings.
Size: 22–24 in.

Mallard
Anas platyrhynchos

The Mallard is the urban duck of the Chicago area—the male's iridescent green head and chestnut breast make this bird easy to identify. This large duck is commonly seen feeding in city parks, small lakes and shallow bays, or in cornfields alongside Canada Geese. With its legs positioned under the middle part of its body, the Mallard walks easily, and it can spring straight out of the water without a running start.

Mallards are the most common duck in North America (and the Northern Hemisphere), and they are easily seen year-round in Chicago. During winter, Mallards are seen banding together in loose flocks in any open water. Birdwatchers habitually scan these groups to test their identification skills. Mallards (like all ducks) molt their feathers, so remember that the distinctive green head of the male Mallard occasionally loses its green pizzazz.

Similar Species: Female resembles many other female dabbling ducks, but look for the blue speculum and her close association with the male Mallard. Male Northern Shoveler (p. 33) has a green head, a white breast and chestnut flanks.

Jan Feb Mar Apr May Jun Jul Aug Sept Oct Nov Dec

Quick I.D.: large duck; bright orange feet; blue speculum bordered by white. *Male:* iridescent green head; bright yellow bill; chestnut breast; white flanks. *Female:* mottled brown; bright orange bill marked with black.
Size: 22–26 in.

Blue-winged Teal
Anas discors

The male Blue-winged Teal has a thin, white crescent on his cheek and a steel blue-gray head to match his inner wing patches. These small ducks are extremely swift flyers, which frustrates their many predators. Their sleek design and rapid wingbeats enable teals to swerve, even at great speeds, and also provide the small ducks the accuracy to make perfectly placed landings. Unlike many ducks that nest pondside, Blue-winged Teals often nest far from water on upland prairies and fallow fields.

Unlike many of the larger dabblers that overwinter in the United States, teals migrate to Central and South America. For this reason, the Blue-winged Teal is often the last duck to arrive in Chicago during spring and the first to leave in fall, usually by the end of September.

Similar Species: Female is easily confused with other female ducks.

Quick I.D.: very small duck; blue forewing; green speculum. *Male:* steel blue head; white crescent on cheek. *Female:* small; plain; yellow-orange legs.
Size: 14–16 in.

Jan Feb Mar Apr May Jun Jul Aug Sept Oct Nov Dec

Northern Shoveler
Anas clypeata

When people start birdwatching, one of their first realizations is that several ducks sport green heads. Other than the Mallard, the Northern Shoveler is one of the easiest to identify—the Northern Shoveler's shovel-like bill stands out among dabbling ducks. The comb-like structures along the bill's edges and its broad, flat shape allow the shoveler to strain small plants and invertebrates from the water's surface or from muddy substrates. A few Northern Shovelers breed in the Chicago area, but most breed farther west.

Many novice birders become interested in birds because they realize the great variety of ducks in their city parks. Some ducks, like the Northern Shoveler, are dabblers that prefer shallow water, are not opposed to roaming around on land and lift straight off the water like a helicopter. Many other ducks in the Chicago area are divers that are found on large lakes. They can be seen running across the water to gain enough speed for flight. Separating the divers from the dabblers is a first step into the wondrous world of waterfowl.

Similar Species: Mallard (p. 31) and all other dabbling ducks lack the combination of a large bill, a white breast and chestnut brown sides.

Jan Feb Mar Apr May Jun Jul Aug Sept Oct Nov Dec

Quick I.D.: mid-sized duck; large bill (longer than head width). *Male:* green head; white breast; chestnut sides. *Female:* mottled brown overall.
Size: 18–20 in.

Ring-necked Duck
Aythya collaris

During the peak of waterfowl migration, Ring-necked Ducks can be quite common on Lake Michigan and all inland lakes. These diving ducks prefer ponds and lakes with muddy bottoms—they dive deeply underwater for aquatic vegetation, including seeds, tubers and pondweed leaves, and invertebrates. Because of their foraging habits, Ring-necked Ducks are susceptible to poisoning from ingesting lead shot. (Wasted shotgun pellets lie at the bottom of many rural wetlands and throughout this duck's summer range across the northern states and Canada.)

Although this duck's name implies the presence of a collar, most experienced birders have given up on seeing this faint feature. The only prominent ring noticeable in field observations is around the tip of the bill, suggesting that a more reasonable name for this bird would have been 'Ring-billed Duck.'

Similar Species: Lesser Scaup (p. 35) and Greater Scaup lack the white shoulder slash and the black back. Female Redhead has a dark brown head to match its body.

Quick I.D.: mid-sized duck; black bill tip; white bill ring. *Male:* dark head with hints of purple; black breast, back and hindquarters; white shoulder slash; gray sides; blue-gray bill with prominent white ring around base. *Female:* dark brown body; light brown head; white eye ring; lighter color closer to bill.
Size: 16–18 in.

Jan Feb Mar Apr May Jun Jul Aug Sept Oct Nov Dec

Lesser Scaup
Aythya affinis

The Lesser Scaup is the Oreo cookie of the duck world—black at both ends and white in the middle. It is a diving duck that prefers deep, open water, and it is common on lakes, harbors and lagoons. As a result of its diving adaptations, the Lesser Scaup is clumsy on land and during take-off, but it gains dignity when it takes to the water. For close-up views, visit the Chicago Botanic Garden or any inland lake in our area.

Because of Chicago's location on Lake Michigan, most species of ducks here are of the diving variety, even though the dabblers are often the most frequently encountered. Diving ducks have smaller wings, which help them dive underwater but make for difficult take-offs and landings. If a duck scoots across the water in an attempt to get airborne, even a first-time birder can tell it's a diver. Divers' legs are placed well back on their bodies—an advantage for underwater swimming—so in order for diving ducks to stand, they must raise their heavy front ends high to maintain balance.

Similar Species: Ring-necked Duck (p. 34) has a white shoulder slash and a black back. Greater Scaup has a green tinge to its head and a long, white stripe on the trailing edge of its wing (seen in flight), and its head lacks the 'bump' on the back of its crown.

Jan Feb Mar Apr May Jun Jul Aug Sept Oct Nov Dec

Quick I.D.: small duck; peaked head. *Male:* dark head with hints of purple; black breast and hindquarters; dirty white sides; grayish back; blue-gray bill; no white breast slash. *Female:* dark brown; well-defined white patch at base of bill.
Size: 15–17 in.

Oldsquaw
Clangula hyemalis

winter

Oldsquaws are tough ducks, lingering in the Chicago area during the harshest time of year—winter. They stop over on Lake Michigan from fall through early spring, during which time their seasonal dress is completely transformed like a photo-negative. The spring breeding plumage of these Arctic-nesting sea ducks is mostly dark with white highlights, while the winter plumage—most frequently seen on our waters—features the opposing characteristics. Regardless of their color, these handsome ducks usually frequent Lake Michigan in rafts a mile or more offshore, limiting observers to brief glimpses of their long, slender tail feathers from Navy Pier, Gillson Park and Waukegan and Racine harbors.

Oldsquaws are among the noisiest breeders on the tundra, their voice is often used to audibly define the Arctic during summer. During their stay here the birds are also vocal, giving the people unable to travel north a taste of Arctic summers. While foraging for minnows, crustaceans and mollusks, Oldsquaws calmly dive to the bottom of our lakes for up to 30 seconds. They are well suited to our winter weather, and the icy pearls of water slide off the bird's body once it resurfaces.

Similar Species: None.

Quick I.D.: mid-sized duck; male has long tail feathers. *Winter male:* white head, flanks, back and underparts; dark cheek, breast and wings. *Winter female:* dark back; light underparts. *Summer male:* dark head, back and neck; white cheek and underparts; pink bill with black base and tip. *Summer female:* light flanks and head; dark cheek.
Size: 17–20 in.

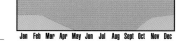

Jan Feb Mar Apr May Jun Jul Aug Sept Oct Nov Dec

Bufflehead
Bucephala albeola

The small, fluffy Bufflehead is perhaps the 'cutest' of Chicago's ducks: its simple plumage and rotund physique bring to mind a child's stuffed toy. During winter, a few Buffleheads are found on just about every lake, particularly off rocky jetties and piers on Lake Michigan.

Because ducks spend most of their lives dripping with water, preening is an important behavior. At the base of the tail of most birds lies the preen (uropygial) gland, which secretes a viscous liquid that inhibits bacterial growth and waterproofs and conditions the feathers. After gently squeezing the preen gland with its bill, a bird can spread the secretion methodically over most of its body, an essential practice to revitalize precious feathers. Sun and wind damage feathers, so it is understandable that birds spend so much time in the preening and maintenance of their feathers.

Similar Species: Male Common Goldeneye (p. 38) is larger and lacks the white, unbordered triangle behind the eye, and the female has a brown head and lacks the cheek patch.

Jan Feb Mar Apr May Jun Jul Aug Sept Oct Nov Dec

Quick I.D.: tiny duck; round body. *Male:* white triangle on back of dark head; white body; dark back. *Female:* dirty brown overall; small, white cheek patch.
Size: 13–15 in.

Common Goldeneye
Bucephala clangula

Although Common Goldeneyes don't breed in the Chicago area, these 'ice ducks' are very common from late fall, through the freezing winter, and right up to their spring migration. Their courtship antics, staged on Lake Michigan and just about every other large waterbody from winter through spring, reinforce a pair's bond before their migration to Canadian woodland lakes.

The courtship display of this widespread duck is one of nature's best slapstick routines. The spry male goldeneye rapidly arches his large, green head back until his bill points skyward, producing a seemingly painful *kraaaagh!* Completely unaffected by this chiropractic wonder, he continuously performs this ritual to mainly disinterested females. The male escalates his spring performance, creating a comedic scene that is most appreciated by birdwatchers.

Similar Species: Bufflehead (p. 37) and Hooded Merganser lack the round, white cheek patch.

Quick I.D.: mid-sized duck. *Male:* large, dark green to black head; round, white cheek patch; white body; black back streaked with white. *Female:* chocolate brown hood; sandy-colored body; orange-brown bill.
Size: 17–19 in.

Jan Feb Mar Apr May Jun Jul Aug Sept Oct Nov Dec

Red-breasted Merganser

Mergus serrator

During spring, Red-breasted Mergansers congregate near the shores of Lake Michigan, initiating their courting rituals prior to their final push north. Males, with their punk-like, slicked crests, ride on the waters while lowering their necks under the surface. With their mid-points submerged, these ducks stare eerily with their wild red eyes, evaluating the females' responses to their actions.

Large, gregarious flocks of Red-breasted Mergansers visit the Great Lakes during migration. However, unlike Common Mergansers, they tend to retreat to coastal waters for winter. During their stay in our waters, their quick 'fly bys' and flashing, white inner wing patches are common features off any lakefront park.

Similar Species: Male Common Merganser (p. 40) lacks the red breast and has white underparts, and the female has a well-defined, reddish-brown hood. Other large ducks and Common Loon (p. 18) all lack the combination of a green head, red bill, red feet and brownish breast.

Quick I.D.: large duck; gray body. *Male:* well-defined, dark green hood; punk-like crest; breast speckled with light brown and black; white collar; brilliant reddish bill and feet; black spinal streak. *Female:* rusty hood blending into white chest. **Size:** 21–25 in.

Jan Feb Mar Apr May Jun Jul Aug Sept Oct Nov Dec

Common Merganser

Mergus merganser

Laboring like a large jumbo jet trying to take off, the Common Merganser runs along the surface of the water, beating its heavy wings until sufficient speed is reached for lift-off. Once in the air, our largest duck looks compressed and arrow-like as it flies strongly in low, straight lines over rivers and lakes.

Mergansers are lean and powerful waterfowl, designed for the underwater pursuit of fish. Unlike the bills of other fish-eating birds, the bill of a merganser is saw-like, serrated to ensure that its squirmy, slimy prey does not escape. In Chicago, Common Mergansers are seen during migration and in winter, when these large ducks congregate in rafts in areas of open water at the mouth of the Chicago River.

Similar Species: Common Loon (p. 18) has a straight dark bill and darker sides. Red-breasted Merganser (p. 39) lacks the white breast and sides.

Quick I.D.: goose-sized. *Male:* well-defined, dark green hood; white body; brilliant reddish-orange bill and feet; black spinal streak.
Female: rusty hood; clean white throat and chin; gray body.
Size: 23–26 in.

Jan Feb Mar Apr May Jun Jul Aug Sept Oct Nov Dec

Ruddy Duck
Oxyura jamaicensis

♀   ♂

breeding

The clowns of freshwater wetlands, male Ruddy Ducks energetically paddle around their breeding wetlands, displaying with great vigor and beating their breasts with their bright blue beaks. The *plap-plap-plap-plap-plap* sound of their display speeds up until its climax: a spasmodic jerk and sputter. The male's performance occurs from April to the middle of June and can occasionally be seen on upland lakes.

Unfortunately, most Ruddy Ducks seen in the Chicago area do not remain to breed. Most courting birds observed in our area continue north to find suitable nesting areas. These birds, however, return in fall and are easily identified not by color but by their unique shape and habits. At this time of year, even the male Ruddy Ducks have lost their ruddy plumage and blue bill, but they maintain their cocky disposition, which seems to be expressed through their permanent smile.

Similar Species: All other waterfowl are generally larger and have shorter tails, relatively smaller heads and longer necks.

Jan Feb Mar Apr May Jun Jul Aug Sept Oct Nov Dec

Quick I.D.: small duck; broad bill; large head; tail often cocked up. *Breeding male:* reddish-brown neck and body; black head and tail; white cheek; blue bill. *Non-breeding male:* dull brown overall; dark cap; white cheek. *Female:* like non-breeding male, but cheek has a dark stripe. **Size:** 14–16 in.

Turkey Vulture
Cathartes aura

Soaring effortlessly above our river valleys and agricultural lands, Turkey Vultures ride rising thermals during their afternoon foraging flights. They seldom need to flap their silver-lined wings, and they rock gently from side to side as they carefully scan fields and shorelines for carcasses. Even at great distances, this bare-headed bird can be identified by the way it tends to hold its wings upwards in a shallow 'V.'

The Turkey Vulture feeds entirely on carrion, which it can sometimes detect by scent alone. Its head is featherless, which is an adaptation to staying clean and parasite-free while it roots around inside carcasses. This king scavenger's well-known habit of regurgitating its rotting meal at intruders might be a defense mechanism: it allows Turkey Vultures to reduce their weight for a quicker take-off, and its smell helps young vultures repel would-be predators.

Similar Species: Hawks, eagles and the Osprey have large, feathered heads and tend to hold their wings flatter in flight, not in a shallow 'V.'

Quick I.D.: larger than a hawk; sexes similar; all black; small, red head. *Immature:* black head. *In flight:* wings held in a shallow 'V'; silver-gray flight feathers; dark wing linings; rocks side to side.
Size: 27–30 in.

Jan Feb Mar Apr May Jun Jul Aug Sept Oct Nov Dec

Cooper's Hawk
Accipiter cooperii

If songbirds dream, the Cooper's Hawk is sure to be the source of their nightmares: Cooper's Hawks terrorize the songbirds living in Chicago's neighborhoods. This mid-sized raptor pursues small birds through forests, maneuvering around leaves and branches in the hope of acquiring prey. Cooper's Hawks take more birds than other accipiters, with small songbirds and the occasional woodpecker being the most numerous prey items.

These small hawks are easy to find darting through European Starling flocks as they pass through our area during their spring and fall migration. During winter, a few of Chicago's wooded neighborhoods have a resident Cooper's Hawk, eager to capture unwary doves, starlings and cardinals. Backyard feeders tend to concentrate favored prey, so they are attractive foraging areas for this small hawk. A sudden eruption of birds off the feeder and a few feathers floating on the wind are often the signs of a sudden, successful Cooper's attack.

Similar Species: Sharp-shinned Hawk is usually smaller, and its tail is squared off and has a thin terminal band. Northern Goshawk is much larger and has white eyebrows.

Jan Feb Mar Apr May Jun Jul Aug Sept Oct Nov Dec

Quick I.D.: smaller than a crow; sexes similar; short, round wings; long tail; blue-gray back; rusty horizontal streaking on underparts; red eyes. *Immature:* brown overall; vertical, brown breast streaks; yellow eyes. *In flight:* flap-and-glide flyer; heavily barred tail is rounded at white tip. **Size:** 15–19 in. (female larger).

Broad-winged Hawk
Buteo platypterus

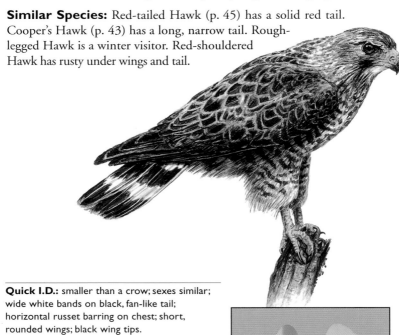

Sighting this mid-sized hawk is a hit-and-miss affair. It is fairly secretive in its wooded breeding habitat, and summers often produce precious few breeding pairs. During migration, however, certain areas, such as the Des Plaines River valley, can produce thousands in a single day! These inconsistencies in observation are not restricted solely to this species, but the Broad-winged Hawk might be the best example of a bird that both frustrates and rewards persistent birders.

Hawks' heavy wings are not designed for continual flapping flight, so these raptors seek out areas that reduce their need to flap. Lake Michigan and the other Great Lakes are daunting to Broad-winged Hawks, which prefer to skirt around the edges, funneling through areas that provide welcome updrafts. Migrating raptors seek out rising thermals created by warm air, or air currents deflecting up from cliffs. The currents help them gain elevation before they launch across a stretch of stagnant, heavy air, giving them longer glides.

Similar Species: Red-tailed Hawk (p. 45) has a solid red tail. Cooper's Hawk (p. 43) has a long, narrow tail. Rough-legged Hawk is a winter visitor. Red-shouldered Hawk has rusty under wings and tail.

Quick I.D.: smaller than a crow; sexes similar; wide white bands on black, fan-like tail; horizontal russet barring on chest; short, rounded wings; black wing tips.
Size: 15–17 in.

Jan Feb Mar Apr May Jun Jul Aug Sept Oct Nov Dec

Red-tailed Hawk
Buteo jamaicensis

With its fierce facial expression and untidy feathers, the Red-tailed Hawk looks as though it has been suddenly and rudely awakened. Its characteristic scream further suggests that the Red-tailed Hawk is a bird best avoided. You would think other birds would treat this large raptor with more respect, but the Red-tailed Hawk is constantly being harassed by crows, jays and blackbirds.

It isn't until this hawk is two or three years old that its tail becomes brick red. The dark head, dark brown 'belt' around its midsection and the dark leading edge to its wings are better field marks because they're seen in most Red-tails. Wherever there is an oak woodlot near open country, it's hard not to spot a Red-tail perched on a post or soaring lazily overhead.

Similar Species: Cooper's Hawk (p. 43) and Sharp-shinned Hawk are smaller, have long tails and rarely soar. Broad-winged Hawk (p. 44) has a banded tail. Northern Harrier has a white rump.

Jan Feb Mar Apr May Jun Jul Aug Sept Oct Nov Dec

Quick I.D.: large hawk; sexes similar; brick red tail (adult only); brown head; variable brown-speckled 'belt'; light flight feathers; dark leading edge to wing lining.
Size: 20–24 in.

American Kestrel
Falco sparverius

This small, noisy falcon is a common summer sight over much of the Chicago area. It has adapted well to modern rural life, and it is commonly seen perched on power lines watching for unwary grasshoppers, birds and rodents. We can also see American Kestrels as we drive off expressways on cloverleaf exits, where the small falcons hover above the long grasses in search of voles and insects.

All falcons are skilled hunters, and they have a unique, tooth-like projection on their hooked bills that can quickly crush the neck of small prey. The American Kestrel's species name, *sparverius,* is Latin for 'pertaining to sparrows,' an occasional prey item. The nests of American Kestrels are often built in abandoned woodpecker cavities. Conservationists have recently discovered that kestrels will use nest boxes when natural cavities are unavailable, which should ensure that these active predators remain common throughout the Chicago area.

Similar Species: Cooper's Hawk (p. 43) and Sharp-shinned Hawk have short, rounded wings. Merlin is larger, has a heavier-streaked breast and lacks the two facial stripes.

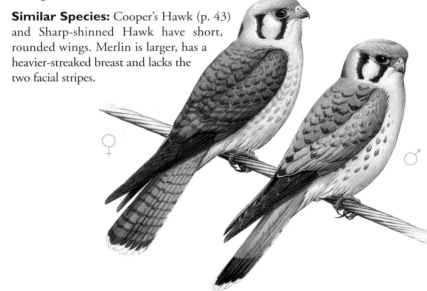

Quick I.D.: smaller than a jay; long, pointed wings; long tail; two vertical black stripes on face; spotted breast; hooked bill. *Male:* blue wings; russet back; colorful head. *Female:* russet back and wings. *In flight:* rapid wingbeat.
Size: 8–9 in.

Jan Feb Mar Apr May Jun Jul Aug Sept Oct Nov Dec

Peregrine Falcon
Falco peregrinus

The Peregrine Falcon is one of the fastest animals in the world, and it can reach speeds of up to 200 m.p.h. Once a Peregrine has its prey singled out, even the fastest ducks and shorebirds have little chance of escaping this effective predator. The Peregrine Falcon plunges on its prey, punching large birds in mid-air and following them to the ground, where they are killed and eaten.

Chicago's Peregrines declined to near extinction because of pesticide residues in the environment. An active recovery plan for this endangered species has restored the population, and this magnificent bird can now be found breeding on downtown skyscrapers. These artificial cliffs seem to duplicate their natural nesting requirements, and the numerous prey species in the area also contribute to their nesting success. It is pleasantly ironic that within some of America's most developed habitats, the noble Peregrine has found sanctuary from possible extinction and can thrill desk-bound executives in their high-rise offices.

Similar Species: American Kestrel (p. 46) and Merlin are much smaller.

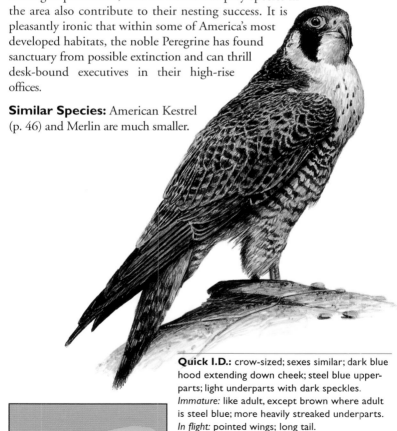

Quick I.D.: crow-sized; sexes similar; dark blue hood extending down cheek; steel blue upperparts; light underparts with dark speckles. *Immature:* like adult, except brown where adult is steel blue; more heavily streaked underparts. *In flight:* pointed wings; long tail.
Size: 15–20 in.

Jan Feb Mar Apr May Jun Jul Aug Sept Oct Nov Dec

Ring-necked Pheasant
Phasianus colchicus

These spectacular birds were introduced from Asia and are now common in the Chicago region. The rooster-like *pe-cok* calls of male pheasants rise from dense, weedy fields, forest preserves and cattail marshes during winter, often surprising leisurely walkers.

During the breeding season, males collect a harem of up to five hens, which they then attempt to protect from the advances of rival males. Males are armed with a short but dangerous spur on the back of the leg, and fights between them can be fierce. Once males have mated with the harem, the females occasionally deposit their eggs into one communal nest. Whether overflowing with multiple clutches or not, pheasant nests are frequently preyed upon by Chicago's coyotes, raccoons and raptors.

Similar Species: None.

Quick I.D.: hawk-sized; long, tapering tail; short, round wings. *Male:* iridescent green hood; fleshy red skin on cheeks; white 'necklace'; golden-red body plumage. *Female:* brown overall.
Size: *Male:* 31–35 in. *Female:* 21–24 in.

Jan Feb Mar Apr May Jun Jul Aug Sept Oct Nov Dec

Black-bellied Plover
Pluvialis squatarola

non-breeding

During spring and fall, Black-bellied Plovers are regularly seen darting along lakefront beaches, grassy openings and plowed fields, foraging with a robin-like run-and-stop technique. Although they dress in plain grays for much of their Chicago stay, Black-bellied Plovers can be seen in their summer tuxedo plumage in early spring and rarely in fall.

Although these plovers are most common in our area during spring and fall migration, a few birds can usually be observed poking around Chicago-area beaches during late summer and winter. Bring your binoculars with you on your next walk—if you're lucky, you might see some Black-bellied Plovers scurrying along the sand ahead of you as they pluck at the surface for food.

Similar Species: American Golden-Plover has a dark cap and lacks the white rump and black wing pits.

Jan Feb Mar Apr May Jun Jul Aug Sept Oct Nov Dec

Quick I.D.: larger than a robin; sexes similar; short, stout, black bill; relatively long, dark legs. *Non-breeding:* slightly streaked, gray body. *In flight:* black wing pits; white rump; white wing linings. **Size:** 11–13 in.

Killdeer

Charadrius vociferus

The Killdeer is probably the most widespread shorebird in the Chicago area. It nests on gravelly shorelines, utility rights-of-way, lawns, pastures and occasionally on gravel roofs in the city. Its name is a paraphrase of its distinctive, loud call—*kill-dee kill-dee kill-deer*—which is a harbinger of spring in our region.

The Killdeer's response to predators relies on deception and good acting skills. To divert a predator's attention away from a nest or a brood of young, an adult Killdeer (like many shorebirds) will flop around to fake an injury, usually a broken wing or leg. Once the Killdeer has the attention of the fox, crow or gull, it leads the predator away from the vulnerable nest. After it reaches a safe distance, the adult Killdeer is suddenly 'healed' and flies off, leaving the predator confused and without a meal.

Similar Species: Semipalmated Plover has only one chest band, is smaller and is found mostly on mudflats.

Quick I.D.: robin-sized; sexes similar; two black bands across breast; brown back; russet rump; long legs; white underparts.
Size: 9–11 in.

Jan Feb Mar Apr May Jun Jul Aug Sept Oct Nov Dec

Lesser Yellowlegs
Tringa flavipes

breeding

On a spring or fall walk along the shores of Lake Michigan, you can see quite a few sandpipers. The Lesser Yellowlegs prefers shallow pools where it can peck for small invertebrates, but it won't hesitate to venture belly-deep into the water to pursue prey. Occasionally, a yellowlegs can be seen hopping along on one leg, with the other one tucked up against the body feathers to reduce heat loss.

Many birders enjoy the challenge of distinguishing the Lesser Yellowlegs from the Greater Yellowlegs. The Greater, which is less common in our area (but don't let that bias your identification), has a relatively longer, heavier bill that is also slightly upturned—so slightly that you notice it one moment and not the next. Generally, the Lesser calls *tew tew*, and the Greater calls *tew tew tew*. Cocky birders will name them at a glance, but more experienced birders will tell you that many of these people are bluffing—much of the time you can only write 'unidentified yellowlegs' in your field notes.

Similar Species: Sanderling (p. 55) and Dunlin (p. 57) are much smaller and have dark legs. Greater Yellowlegs is larger and has a longer, two-toned bill generally two or three times the length of its head.

Jan Feb Mar Apr May Jun Jul Aug Sept Oct Nov Dec

Quick I.D.: robin-sized; sexes similar; long, bright yellow legs; finely streaked gray body; bill shorter than head length.
Size: 9–11 in.

Solitary Sandpiper
Tringa solitaria

True to its name, the Solitary Sandpiper is frequently seen alone or in small groups along the shores of Lake Michigan, mudflats and the edges of inland lakes and rivers. This antisocial behavior is fairly unusual among migrating shorebirds in our area, but it is this bird's habit of bobbing its body like a Latin dancer that is its most striking feature.

Solitary Sandpipers stalk shorelines, picking up aquatic invertebrates, such as waterboatmen and damselfly nymphs. Unlike most other shorebirds, these northern breeders have been known to cleverly stir the water with a foot to spook out prey.

Although Chicago-area birdwatchers will see far more of other types of shorebirds in a year, the Solitary Sandpiper is encountered frequently in our area during migration. Its voice is a high, thin *peet-wheet* or *wheet wheet wheet* during its spring passage.

Similar Species: Lesser Yellowlegs (p. 51) has bright yellow legs and no eye ring. Spotted Sandpiper (p. 53) has an incomplete eye ring, a very spotted breast and an orange, black-tipped bill.

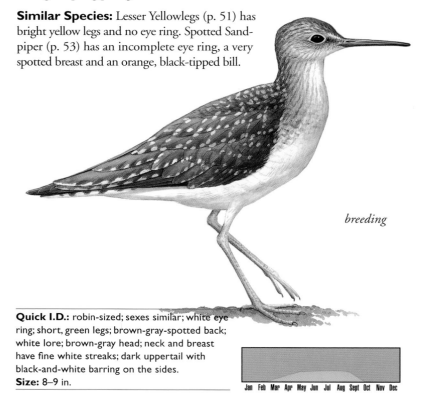

breeding

Quick I.D.: robin-sized; sexes similar; white eye ring; short, green legs; brown-gray-spotted back; white lore; brown-gray head; neck and breast have fine white streaks; dark uppertail with black-and-white barring on the sides.
Size: 8–9 in.

Jan Feb Mar Apr May Jun Jul Aug Sept Oct Nov Dec

Spotted Sandpiper
Actitis macularia

This common shorebird of lakes and rivers has a most uncommon mating strategy. In a reversal of the gender roles of most birds, the female Spotted Sandpiper competes for males in spring. After the nest is built and the eggs are laid, the female leaves to find another mate, while the first male is left to incubate the eggs. This behavior can be repeated two or more times before the female settles down with one male to raise her last brood of chicks. Spotted Sandpipers nest in the Chicago area, and they are frequently encountered during summer and the migratory months along the undisturbed shores and rocky piers of Lake Michigan and inland wetlands and ponds.

The Spotted Sandpiper is readily identified by its arthritic-looking, stiff-winged flight low over water. Its peppy call—*eat-wheat wheat-wheat-wheat*—bursts from startled birds as they retreat from shoreline disturbances. Spotted Sandpipers constantly teeter and bob when not in flight, which makes them easy to identify.

Similar Species: Killdeer (p. 50) has dark throat bands. Solitary Sandpiper (p. 52) has an eye ring and lacks the prominent breast spots. Lesser Yellowlegs (p. 51) has longer legs.

breeding

Quick I.D.: smaller than a robin; sexes similar; often teeters and bobs; yellow legs. *Breeding:* spotted breast; olive-gray back; yellow bill tipped with black. *Female:* spots more pronounced.
Size: 7–8 in.

Jan Feb Mar Apr May Jun Jul Aug Sept Oct Nov Dec

Ruddy Turnstone
Arenaria interpres

During migration, striking, harlequin-faced Ruddy Turnstones prefer sandy and pebbly beaches all along Lake Michigan's shoreline. They can be seen on jetties and beaches, where they often are seen in good numbers mixed in with other species of shorebirds. Turnstones probe in the wet sand and between small rocks for amphipods, isopods and other small invertebrates that live buried along the shoreline.

Ruddy Turnstones do much of their foraging by probing, but they have gained fame for an unusual feeding technique. As the name implies, the turnstone flips over small rocks and debris with its bill to expose hidden invertebrates. The turnstone's bill is short, stubby and slightly upturned—ideal for this foraging style.

Similar Species: Dunlin (p. 57) has a downcurved bill and lacks the bold patterning.

breeding

Quick I.D.: robin-sized; sexes similar (female slightly paler); white belly; black bib; stout, slightly upturned bill; orange-red legs.
Breeding: ruddy upperparts; white face, black collar; gray crown. *Non-breeding:* dark brownish upperparts and face.
Size: 9–10 in.

Jan Feb Mar Apr May Jun Jul Aug Sept Oct Nov Dec

Sanderling
Calidris alba

A spring or fall stroll along a sandy beach on Lake Michigan is often punctuated by the sight of these tiny runners, which seem to enjoy nothing more than playing in the surf. Sanderlings are characteristically seen chasing and retreating from the rolling waves, never getting caught in the charging water. Only the Sanderling commonly forages in this manner, plucking at the exposed invertebrates stirred up by the wave action. Without waves to chase along calm shorelines, Sanderlings unenthusiastically probe into wet soil in much the same fashion as many other sandpipers.

This sandpiper is one of the world's most widespread birds. It breeds across the Arctic in Alaska, Canada and Russia, and it spends winter running up and down sandy shorelines in North America, South America, Asia, Africa and Australia.

Similar Species: Least Sandpiper (p. 56) is smaller and darker. Dunlin (p. 57) is darker and has a downcurved bill.

breeding

Jan Feb Mar Apr May Jun Jul Aug Sept Oct Nov Dec

Quick I.D.: smaller than a robin; straight, black bill; dark legs. *Breeding:* rusty head and breast. *Non-breeding:* white underparts; grayish-white upperparts.
Size: 7¹/₂–8¹/₂ in.

Least Sandpiper
Calidris minutilla

non-breeding

The Least Sandpiper is the smallest of the shorebirds, but its size is not a deterrent to its migratory feats. Like most other 'peeps'—a term used to group the nearly indistinguishable *Calidris* sandpipers—the Least Sandpipers passing through Chicago migrate to the Arctic to breed.

Groups of these tiny birds can be spotted against the damp sands of beaches, mudflats and lakeshores throughout our area. Their plumage matches perfectly their preferred habitat, and it is usually their rapid movements that reveal these diminutive sprinters. Least Sandpipers tenaciously peck the moist substrate with their dexterous bills, eating mosquitoes, beach fleas, amphipods and other aquatic invertebrates.

Similar Species: Other 'peeps' tend to have dark legs and are generally larger. Pectoral Sandpiper is larger and has a well-defined pectoral border.

Quick I.D.: sparrow-sized; sexes similar; black bill; yellow legs; dark, mottled back; buff-brown breast, head and nape; light breast streaking. *Immature:* like adult, but with fainter breast streaking.
Size: 5–6 in.

Jan Feb Mar Apr May Jun Jul Aug Sept Oct Nov Dec

Dunlin
Calidris alpina

The flocking behavior of these small, plump shorebirds is a spectacular performance. Dunlins are communal creatures, and as they pass Chicago they form a swirling cloud of individuals flying wing tip to wing tip, instantaneously changing course, hundreds behaving as if one entity. These hypnotic flights, flashing alternating shades of white and black, are occasionally seen as Dunlins migrate along Lake Michigan's shores. The flocks move both northward and southward during their trips around Lake Michigan shorelines. These tight flocks are generally more exclusive than many other shorebird troupes: few species mix with groups of Dunlins.

The Dunlin, like many other shorebirds, nests on the Arctic tundra and winters on the coasts of North America, Europe and Asia. It was originally called a 'Dunling' (meaning 'a small brown bird'), but for reasons lost to science the 'g' was later dropped.

Similar Species: Least Sandpiper (p. 56) is smaller. Sanderling (p. 55) is paler and is usually seen running in the surf.

breeding

Quick I.D.: smaller than a robin; sexes similar; slightly downcurved bill; dark legs. *Breeding:* black belly; streaked underparts; rusty back. *Non-breeding:* pale gray underparts; grayish-brown upperparts.
Size: 8–9 in.

Jan Feb Mar Apr May Jun Jul Aug Sept Oct Nov Dec

Short-billed Dowitcher
Limnodromus griseus

When cool fall air descends from the north, shorebirds concentrate along muddy and flooded fields. The oncoming winter forces dowitchers and other shorebirds to retreat to the south, often packing them together in large numbers along the way. Dowitchers tend to be stockier than most of their neighboring shorebirds, and they avoid deeper water. The sewing machine–like rhythm with which dowitchers forage deeply into the mudflats is helpful for field identification.

Unfortunately, separating the two Chicago-area dowitcher species is one of the most difficult tasks any birder can attempt. Although most people are perfectly content to simply call them 'dowitchers,' some birders insist they can separate the two species by voice alone (Short-billed: *tu tu tu*; Long-billed: *keek*).

Similar Species: Common Snipe (p. 59) has longer legs, heavily barred upperparts and different foraging techniques. Long-billed Dowitcher has barring on its sides and an unmarked breast, its plumage is darker overall, and its bill is slightly longer.

non-breeding

Quick I.D.: larger than a robin; sexes similar; very long, straight, dark bill; very stocky body; short neck. *Breeding:* reddish underparts; lightly barred flanks; dark, mottled upperparts; dark eye line; light eyebrow; dark yellow legs; white rump. *Non-breeding:* gray overall; white belly.
Size: 11–12¹⁄₂ in. (female larger).

| Jan | Feb | Mar | Apr | May | Jun | Jul | Aug | Sept | Oct | Nov | Dec |

Common Snipe
Gallinago gallinago

These shorebirds are both secretive and well camouflaged, so few people notice them until the birds fly suddenly out of nearby grassy tussocks. As soon as snipes take to the air, they perform a series of quick zigzags, an evasive maneuver designed to confuse predators. The in-flight movements are so effective that, in times past, only the best shorebird hunters were known as 'snipers'—a term later adopted by the military. Snipes are seldom seen in large groups, nor are they normally encountered along open shorelines; their heavily streaked plumage is suited to grassy habitat.

The mystical 'winnowing' sound of courting Common Snipes is heard infrequently in the Chicago area, because their breeding habitat has largely been destroyed. However, during spring evenings at sedge meadows in Illinois Beach and Chain O'Lakes state parks, the accelerating sound, produced in flight by air passing through spread tail feathers, can thrill perceptive observers.

Similar Species: All other shorebirds are either too short of bill or not as heavily streaked.

Jan Feb Mar Apr May Jun Jul Aug Sept Oct Nov Dec

Quick I.D.: robin-sized; sexes similar; long, black-tipped bill; heavily streaked back; short neck; striped head; long legs.
Size: 10¹/₂–11¹/₂ in.

American Woodcock
Scolopax minor

For much of the year, the American Woodcock's behavior matches its cryptic and unassuming attire. This well-camouflaged bird inhabits woods and thickets—its lifestyle does little to reveal it to the outside world.

For a short month each spring, male woodcocks explode into vanity. The courtship performance begins when the male selects a clearing in the woods, where he gives a plaintive *bjeent* that inspires him into an Elvis-like boogie. The woodcock's legs are short, so he usually selects a stage that is free of thick vegetation, which would block the females' views of his swinging strut. When he has sashayed sufficiently, he takes to the air. Spiraling upward into the evening sky, he twitters increasingly toward the sky-dance climax. Upon hitting the peak of his ascent, the male woodcock relaxes and then plummets, uncontrolled, to the ground. Just before striking the ground, the woodcock pulls out of the crippled dive and alights on his dancing stage, where he resumes his breeding ballet. To attend this long-running performance, visit a moist, open woodland, such as Cuba Marsh or Illinois Beach State Park, in April or May.

Similar Species: Common Snipe (p. 59) has a striped head and back and pointed wings.

Quick I.D.: jay-sized; sexes similar; chunky; very long bill; large eyes; rusty underparts.
In flight: rounded wings.
Size: 10–12 in.

Jan Feb Mar Apr May Jun Jul Aug Sept Oct Nov Dec

Bonaparte's Gull
Larus philadelphia

The scratchy little calls of Bonaparte's Gulls accompany these migrants as they forage along Chicago's shorelines. These gulls commonly feed on the water's surface, and they can often be seen resting atop the water or circling around inland lakes and flooded fields. Bonaparte's Gulls pass through our area during the last two weeks of April and the first half of May on their way north to breed in the northern boreal forest. There they nest, in most un-gull-like fashion, in spruce trees.

After the summer breeding season, most Bonaparte's Gulls lose their distinctive black hoods, but they retain flashy white wing patches and a noticeable black spot behind the eyes. When they return to our area from September through December, they are more visible, but far less striking in appearance. This gull was named not after the famed French emperor, but after his nephew, Charles Lucien Bonaparte, who brought recognition to his family's name through the practice of ornithology.

Similar Species: Common Tern (p. 64) has a forked tail and lacks a white wing flash.

breeding

Jan Feb Mar Apr May Jun Jul Aug Sept Oct Nov Dec

Quick I.D.: small gull; sexes similar; black bill; dark eyes. *Breeding:* black hood. *Non-breeding:* white head with dark ear spot. *In flight:* wing tips have black outline; wings flash white.
Size: 12–14 in.

Ring-billed Gull
Larus delawarensis

breeding

This widespread, extremely common gull is slightly smaller than the Herring Gull and has a distinctive dark bill ring, for which it is well named. The Ring-billed Gull is frequently seen in parks and shopping center parking lots. The warm air rising from concrete and asphalt are like elevators that dozens of gulls ride simultaneously, climbing until their sleek shapes vanish into the sky.

Although these gulls seem to be regular urbanites, like so many people in Chicago, they commute daily into the city. From shoreline suburbs, gull traffic can be seen during early mornings, congested along skyways leading into town. Their daily activities involve squabbling with other greedy gulls over leftovers from fast-food restaurants and for food in open areas. When nicely fed, they might break from feeding duties by soaring high above the hectic pace of city life.

Similar Species: Herring Gull (p. 63) is larger, has pink legs and lacks the bill ring. Bonaparte's Gull (p. 61) is smaller and has a black head in spring and a white wing flash.

Quick I.D.: mid-sized gull; sexes similar; black ring near bill tip; yellow bill and legs; gray back and wing coverts; light eyes; black wing tips; small, white spots on black primaries; white underparts. *Non-breeding:* white head and nape washed with brown. *First winter:* mottled grayish brown; brown band on white tail.
Size: 18–20 in.

Jan Feb Mar Apr May Jun Jul Aug Sept Oct Nov Dec

Herring Gull
Larus argentatus

Many gulls come and go in Chicago, but the Herring Gull is a year-round resident in the Great Lakes region. This familiar bird is called a 'sea gull,' but it does not rightfully deserve that name, because the Herring Gulls seen in our area rarely venture to salt water. If this bird were to relinquish the title, however, it would likely be labeled with one even less desirable. Large flocks of Herring Gulls can be found in bays, lakes, garbage dumps, shorelines, city parks and agricultural fields, and they are mistakenly thought of as dirty birds. Herring Gulls are so widely distributed they are sure to be sighted on just about any birding trip taken along the shore of Lake Michigan.

Although often overlooked by even the most curious naturalist, the Herring Gull is an engineering marvel. Agile on land, an effortless flyer, wonderfully adaptive and with a stomach for anything digestible, Herring Gulls are perhaps the most widely distributed gull in North America.

Similar Species: Ring-billed Gull (p. 62) has yellow legs and a black-banded bill.

breeding

Jan Feb Mar Apr May Jun Jul Aug Sept Oct Nov Dec

Quick I.D.: hawk-sized; sexes similar; white head and body; gray back; pink legs; dark wing tips; yellow eyes; red spot on lower mandible. *Immature:* variable; brown overall; all-black tail. **Size:** 24–26 in.

Common Tern
Sterna hirundo

breeding

The Common Tern generally goes unnoticed until a splash draws attention to its headfirst dives into water. Once it has firmly seized a small fish in its black-tipped bill, the tern bounces back into the air and continues its leisurely flight. Common Terns are easily observed in May, working the shores of Lake Michigan during migration. Although some remain to nest on sandbars and unvegetated islands just inland from Lake Michigan, most choose to continue north for breeding opportunities.

Although terns and gulls share many of the same physical characteristics, there are features that clearly separate the two groups. Terns seldom rest on the water, and they rarely soar in flight. They also have very short necks, pointed wings and long, forked tails, and they tend to look toward the ground during flight. Both gulls and terns tend to nest in similar regions, but this might be more convenient for the gulls, because they routinely prey on the smaller terns.

Similar Species: Caspian Tern has a large, red bill and is gull-sized. Forster's Tern has a longer, gray tail and frosted wing tips.

Quick I.D.: larger than a pigeon; sexes similar; black cap; red bill tipped with black; gray back and wings; pointed wings; white throat; light gray belly; light grayish tail. *In flight:* light grayish, forked tail; often hovers.

Size: 14–16 in.

Jan Feb Mar Apr May Jun Jul Aug Sept Oct Nov Dec

Black Tern
Chlidonias niger

Over cattail marshes, the erratic, aeronautic flight of the Black Tern is unmatched by any other bird. It dips and dives, swoops and spins in dizzying foraging flights, picking insects neatly off the water's surface and in mid-air. This tern is the master of the airways above its marshy breeding grounds, breaking only briefly to perch on a nearby post or return to its nest.

Black Terns build their nests near the cattails and vegetated islands of Lake Calumet and other marshes in our region. They nest on floating platforms or small islands. Both the male and female incubate the clutch of two to four eggs and help feed the quickly growing young.

Black Terns look like frail birds, but they are built to have dominion over the winds. When they leave our area in September, they head out to tropical coasts, to dance over foreign waters until their spring return.

Similar Species: Common Tern (p. 64) and Forster's Tern are much lighter underneath.

breeding

Jan Feb Mar Apr May Jun Jul Aug Sept Oct Nov Dec

Quick I.D.: robin-sized; sexes similar; gray upperparts and tail; black bill; long, pointed wings; shallowly forked tail; reddish-black legs. *Breeding:* black head, neck and underparts; white undertail coverts. *Non-breeding:* white underparts; black mark behind eye; dark gray collar on sides in front of wings.
Size: 9–11 in.

Rock Dove
Columba livia

This Eurasian native was first brought to North America in 1606 as a food source. Rock Doves were to receive the last laugh, though, because they quickly dispersed from the East Coast to colonize the entire continent. The Rock Dove (or pigeon) has taken advantage of humans for food and shelter: it lives in old buildings, on ledges and on bridges, and it feeds primarily on waste grain and human handouts. Nowhere is this bird more common than in the steep-walled canyons of Chicago's skyscrapers.

Rock Doves might appear strained when walking—their heads move back and forth with every step—but few birds are as agile in flight or as abundant in urban and industrial areas. While no other bird varies as much in coloration, all Rock Doves, whether white, red, blue or mixed-pigment, will clap their wings above and below their bodies upon take-off.

Similar Species: Mourning Dove (p. 67) is the same length as the Rock Dove, but it is slender and has a long, tapering tail and olive-brown plumage.

Quick I.D.: mid-sized pigeon; sexes similar; variable color (iridescent blue-gray, black, red or white); white rump (usually); orange feet; fleshy base to bill.
Size: 13–14 in.

Jan Feb Mar Apr May Jun Jul Aug Sept Oct Nov Dec

Mourning Dove
Zenaida macroura

Mourning Doves are frequently seen commuting to and from communal roost sites in evergreen woodlands. The Mourning Dove is a swift, direct flyer, and its wings can be heard whistling through the air. When not in flight, the peaceful *cooooo-cooooo-coooooah* call of the Mourning Dove can be heard filtering through open woodlands. These year-round residents roost inconspicuously in trees, but their soft cooing often betrays their presence.

The Mourning Dove feeds primarily on the ground, picking up grain and grit in open areas and visiting many backyard feeders in our region. It builds a flat, loose stick nest that rests flimsily on branches and trunks. Mourning Doves are attentive parents, and, like other members of the pigeon family, they feed 'milk' to their young. It isn't true milk—birds lack mammary glands—but a fluid produced by glands in the bird's crop. The chicks insert their bills down the adult's throat to eat the thick liquid.

Similar Species: Rock Dove (p. 66) has a white rump, is stockier and has a shorter tail.

Jan Feb Mar Apr May Jun Jul Aug Sept Oct Nov Dec

Quick I.D.: jay-sized; sexes similar; gray-brown plumage; long, white-trimmed, tapering tail; sleek body; dark, shiny patch below ear; orange feet; dark bill; peach-colored underparts.
Size: 11–13 in.

Monk Parakeet
Myiopsitta monachus

Monk Parakeets occur as startling, unexpected flashes of green flying through the concrete jungle in the heart of Chicago. Such tropical sights seem oddly placed, but Monk Parakeet colonies have been thriving since the late 1970s here in our area. This introduced species, originally from South America, is quite ironically one of the few birds that residents living in the depths of Chicago's urban maze can view regularly.

Such circumstances raise questions about how these birds arrived and withstood our challenging environment. Monk Parakeets were released, or escaped as captive birds, and soon began to colonize local areas. Their nests, haystacks of sticks, are used throughout the year and shield the birds from temperatures that dip far below zero. Because there are few natural food sources, Monk Parakeets depend on the generosity of human neighbors and ornamental plants to supply them with a year-round supply of food. It is inspiring to think that these tropical flying jewels have happened to select one of America's most altered environments to bring to us a sense of wildness.

Similar Species: None.

Quick I.D.: larger than a jay; sexes similar; green upperparts, wings and tail; heavy, yellow, hooked bill; grayish face and throat; bluish flight feathers; yellow-green belly.
Size: 11 1/2 in.

Jan Feb Mar Apr May Jun Jul Aug Sept Oct Nov Dec

Eastern Screech-Owl

Otus asio

Despite its small size, the Eastern Screech-Owl is an adaptable hunter. It has a varied diet that ranges from insects, earthworms and fish to birds larger than itself. Silent and reclusive by day, screech-owls hunt at night.

Some owls' senses are refined for darkness and their bodies for silence: their large, forward-facing eyes have many times more light-gathering sensors than do ours, and the wings of nocturnal owls are edged with soft, frayed feathers for silent flight. Their ears, located on the sides of their heads, are asymmetrical (one is higher than the other), which enables these birds to track sounds more easily. Given these adaptations, it is no surprise that owls have successfully invaded nearly all of the world's major ecosystems.

gray phase

A birder with a keen ear, while strolling along the wooded paths of ravines, river valleys and hardwood forests during early spring evenings, will hear the distinctive whistled voice of the Eastern Screech-Owl. The call's rhythm has often been compared to that of a bouncing ball coming to rest.

Similar Species: Northern Saw-whet Owl has a dark facial disc and no ear tufts, and its call does not increase in pace.

Jan Feb Mar Apr May Jun Jul Aug Sept Oct Nov Dec

Quick I.D.: robin-sized; sexes similar; short, widely spaced ear tufts; heavy vertical streaking and bars on chest; yellow eyes; dark bill; two color phases (gray, which is more common, and red).

Size: 8–9 in. (female slightly larger).

Great Horned Owl

Bubo virginianus

The Great Horned Owl is the most widely distributed owl in North America, and it is among the most formidable of predators. It uses specialized hearing, powerful talons and human-sized eyes during nocturnal hunts for mice, rabbits, quails, amphibians and occasionally fish. It has a poorly developed sense of smell, however, which is why it can prey on skunks—worn-out and discarded Great Horned Owl feathers are often identifiable by a simple sniff.

The deep, resonant hooting of the Great Horned Owl is easily imitated, often leading to interesting exchanges between bird and birder. The call's deep tone is not as distinctive as its pace, which closely follows the rhythm of *Eat my food, I'll-eat yooou*. The calls and the bird's distinctive silhouette can even be encountered at night in Chicago-area subdivisions.

Similar Species: Eastern Screech-Owl (p. 69) is much smaller and has vertical breast streaking. Long-eared Owl has a slimmer body and vertical streaks on its chest, and its ear tufts are very close together.

Quick I.D.: hawk-sized; sexes similar; large, widely spaced ear tufts; fine, horizontal chest bars; dark brown plumage; white throat.
Size: 18–25 in.

Jan Feb Mar Apr May Jun Jul Aug Sept Oct Nov Dec

Common Nighthawk
Cordeiles minor

The Common Nighthawk, which is unrelated to true hawks, has a Dr. Jekyll and Mr. Hyde split personality. Mild-mannered by day, it rests on the ground or on a horizontal tree branch, its color and shape blending perfectly into the texture of the bark. At dusk, the Common Nighthawk takes on a new form as a dazzling and erratic flyer, catching insects in flight.

To many people, the sound of the nighthawk is the sound of summer evenings, when the birds leave their gravel rooftop nests to court over the city. The nighthawks repeatedly call out with a loud, nasal *peeent* as they circle high overhead, then they dive suddenly toward the ground and create a hollow *vroom* sound by thrusting their wings forward at the last possible moment, pulling out of the dive.

Similar Species: Whip-poor-will (p. 72) and Chuck-will's-widow have rounded wings and tails.

♂

Jan Feb Mar Apr May Jun Jul Aug Sept Oct Nov Dec

Quick I.D.: robin-sized; sexes similar; cryptic, light to dark brown plumage. *Male:* white throat. *Female:* buff throat. *In flight:* shallowly forked tail; long, pointed wings; white wrist bands; flight is erratic.
Size: 9–10 in.

Whip-poor-will

Caprimulgus vociferus

Although heard far more often than it is seen, the Whip-poor-will makes identification easy for novice birdwatchers because this nighttime hunter fills evenings with its own name. The distinctive *whip-poor-will* is chanted persistently at the rate of about once per second. At prime Whip-poor-will sites, such as Indiana Dunes and Illinois Beach state parks, these birds sing continuously from dusk to dawn.

The Whip-poor-will arrives in the Chicago area by the end of April and soon finds an open woodland in which to nest. No nest is constructed; rather, the eggs are simply laid on bare ground. These well-camouflaged birds also choose to roost during the day on bare ground, and at dusk they can occasionally be seen resting on or alongside roadsides.

The Iroquois were obviously respectful of these birds, because, according to legend, the flowers of wild moccasin plants were thought to be the shoes of Whip-poor-wills.

Similar Species: Common Nighthawk (p. 71) has pointed wings, a notched tail and white wrist bands.

Quick I.D.: robin-sized; gray-brown plumage; wings and tail rounded; black throat; light outer tail feathers; light 'necklace'. *Male:* white outer tail feathers and 'necklace'. *Female:* buff 'necklace' and outer tail feathers.
Size: 9–10 in.

Jan Feb Mar Apr May Jun Jul Aug Sept Oct Nov Dec

Belted Kingfisher

Ceryle alcyon

Where open water is found in the Chicago area, Belted Kingfishers can be encountered every day of the year, crashing into calm waters in search of fish. A dead branch extending over water will often serve as a perch from which to survey the fish below, which they catch with precise headfirst dives. Although there are many species of kingfisher in the world, the Belted Kingfisher is the only member of its family across most of the United States.

The Belted Kingfisher builds its nest near the end of a long tunnel excavated a few feet into sandy or dirt banks. A rattling call, like a teacup shaking on a saucer, is likely more useful in finding these birds than their trademark plumage. With most birds, the males are more colorful, but female kingfishers are distinguished from males by the presence of a second, rust-colored band across the belly.

Similar Species: None.

Jan Feb Mar Apr May Jun Jul Aug Sept Oct Nov Dec

Quick I.D.: pigeon-sized; blue-gray back, wings and head; shaggy crest; heavy bill. *Male:* single, blue chest band. *Female:* blue chest band; rust-colored 'belt'.
Size: 12–14 in.

Red-headed Woodpecker
Melanerpes erythrocephalus

'His tri-coloured plumage, so striking. ... A gay and frolicsome disposition, diving and vociferating around the high dead limbs of some large tree, amusing the passenger with their gambols.'

—Alexander Wilson

When Wilson landed in North America, the Scotsman, with little money and few skills, did not know what he'd do in the New World. Like a revelation, a Red-headed Woodpecker was one of the first birds to greet the immigrant. Never had Wilson seen such beauty, and the bird inspired the future 'father of American ornithology' to devote his life to birds. With no formal ornithological background, he went on to discover and describe dozens of North American species. Although the Red-headed Woodpecker's plumage might not drive everyone to great scientific achievements, look for these wondrous beauties at Illinois Beach or Indiana Dunes state parks and become impassioned by their beauty.

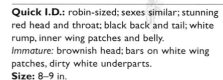

Similar Species: Red-bellied Woodpecker (p. 75) has a gray cheek and black-and-white zebra stripes on its back.

Quick I.D.: robin-sized; sexes similar; stunning red head and throat; black back and tail; white rump, inner wing patches and belly.
Immature: brownish head; bars on white wing patches, dirty white underparts.
Size: 8–9 in.

Jan Feb Mar Apr May Jun Jul Aug Sept Oct Nov Dec

Red-bellied Woodpecker
Melanerpes carolinus

♂

An unexpected barking *churr* in mixed woodlands anywhere in our area is often the first
clue that the oddly named Red-bellied
Woodpecker is about. A fairly common
resident in our area, this woodpecker
mysteriously acquired a name that
reflects a very subtle field mark.
Since the 'Red-headed' name is
granted to a more deserving
woodpecker, perhaps the
most suitable name would
have been the 'Zebra-backed
Woodpecker.'

♀

Regardless of its unusual name,
this woodpecker has recently en-
joyed a slight increase in population in our area.
Although the Red-bellied Woodpecker is continually
threatened by bullying European Starlings, the regeneration of
Midwestern forests has encouraged the dispersal of these birds. Interestingly,
birdfeeders have also played a role in their recent successes by increasing their
survival through our winters. Many Chicago birdwatchers fondly remember
the chilly winter day when this striking bird first visited their suet or sunflower seed feeder. Although the seed source might be completely reliable
throughout the cold months, Red-bellied Woodpeckers take no chances, and
hoard the food, filling tree cavities, gaps in shingles and other small spaces
with insurance seeds.

Similar Species: Red-headed Woodpecker (p. 74) has a solid red head and
a solid black upper back. Northern Flicker (p. 78) has black spotting on its
underparts, yellow wing and tail linings and lacks the black-and-white barring
on the back.

Jan Feb Mar Apr May Jun Jul Aug Sept Oct Nov Dec

Quick I.D.: robin-sized; black-and-white barring
on back; red crown and nape; plain gray face and
underparts; very faint red belly; white rump.
Male: red forehead. *Female:* gray forehead.
Size: 9 in.

Downy Woodpecker
Picoides pubescens

Soft taps carry through a quiet forest, sounding out the activities of a Downy Woodpecker. It searches for hidden invertebrates methodically, by chipping off dead bark and probing into crevices. The woodpecker's small bill is amazingly effective at removing tiny slabs of bark, which rain down to the forest floor. Often, it is only when all the nooks of a tree have been probed that the Downy will look about and give a chip note before moving on to explore neighboring trees.

The Downy Woodpecker is a systematic forager, and because of its small bill, it can find food where larger-billed woodpeckers cannot reach. This black-and-white bird is the smallest North American woodpecker and is common throughout our area. It's easily attracted to backyard feeders by suet. The male is readily distinguished from the female by a small patch of red feathers on the back of its head.

Similar Species: Hairy Woodpecker (p. 77) is larger and it has a longer bill and clean white outer tail feathers.

Quick I.D.: large sparrow–sized; black-and-white wings and back; unmarked, white underparts; short, stubby bill; white outer tail feathers are spotted black. *Male:* red patch on back of head. *Female:* no red patch.
Size: 6–7 in.

Jan Feb Mar Apr May Jun Jul Aug Sept Oct Nov Dec

Hairy Woodpecker
Picoides villosus

The Hairy Woodpecker looks like an overgrown Downy Woodpecker, and it shares the habitat of its smaller cousin. Although not as common nor as easily approached as the Downy, the Hairy's loud calls and hammering enliven a winter forest. Its long, dark bill hammers rotting wood apart, exposing the soft-bodied larval invertebrates inside. Many woodpeckers are dependent on dead and dying trees for nest sites and stable food sources. The human perception that dead wood and old trees are waste is a view not shared by many species of woodpecker.

Although Hairy Woodpeckers can be encountered every day of the year in the Chicago area, they are more frequently encountered in winter, when the leaves are off the trees and the birds are busy feeding. This mid-sized woodpecker can be often encountered foraging diligently in oak woodlots and riparian river bottoms along the Des Plaines River.

Similar Species: Downy Woodpecker (p. 76) is smaller and has a shorter bill. Red-headed Woodpecker (p. 74) has an all-red head.

Quick I.D.: smaller than a robin; black-and-white back and wings; white underparts; bill is as long as head is wide; no black spots on white outer tail feathers. *Male:* red patch on back of head. *Female:* no red patch.
Size: 8–9 in.

Jan Feb Mar Apr May Jun Jul Aug Sept Oct Nov Dec

WOODPECKERS 77

Northern Flicker

Colaptes auratus

Walkers strolling through Lincoln Park might be surprised by a woodpecker flushing from the ground before them. As the Northern Flicker beats a hasty retreat, it reveals an unmistakable white rump and yellow wing linings. It is the least arboreal of our woodpeckers, and it spends more time feeding on the ground than other woodpeckers. Often it is only when the Northern Flicker is around its nest cavity in a tree that it truly behaves like other woodpeckers: clinging, rattling and drumming.

The Northern Flicker can easily be seen all year in our area, and it visits back-yard feeders particularly during winter. The Northern Flicker (and other birds) squash ants and then preen themselves with the remains. Ants contain concentrations of formic acid, which is believed to kill small parasites living on the flicker's skin and in its feathers.

Similar Species: Red-bellied Woodpecker (p. 75) has a red crown and black-and-white stripes on its back.

Quick I.D.: jay-sized; brown-barred back; spotted underparts; black bib; white rump; long bill; yellow wing and tail feathers; gray crown; red nape. *Male:* black mustache. *Female:* no mustache.
Size: 11–14 in.

Jan Feb Mar Apr May Jun Jul Aug Sept Oct Nov Dec

Ruby-throated Hummingbird

Archilochus colubris

Everyone knows and loves the tiny hummingbird that buzzes into flowerbeds and visits special feeders throughout summer. These miniature birds span the ecological gap between birds and insects, feeding on the energy-rich nectar that flower blooms provide in exchange for the feeder's pollinating assistance. Perhaps it is the bird's remarkable size, or its intimate association with flowers, that make smiles appear whenever these birds are discussed.

The Ruby-throated Hummingbird is the only bird of its kind to uncommonly breed in the Chicago area. As such, it is interesting to look at this species and admire one of nature's engineering marvels. Weighing about the same as a quarter, hummingbirds are capable of speeds of up to 60 m.p.h.! In straight-ahead flight they beat their wings up to 80 times per second (slightly less if hovering or reversing), and in migration they cross the Gulf of Mexico, an incredible non-stop journey of over 620 miles. Although impressive, the astonishing intricacy and sophistication possessed by the Ruby-throated Hummingbird may be overshadowed by the inescapable joy carried by this bird upon its tiny wings.

Similar Species: None.

Jan Feb Mar Apr May Jun Jul Aug Sept Oct Nov Dec

Quick I.D.: our smallest bird; iridescent green back, long, thin, dark bill; light underparts; dark tail. *Male:* iridescent red throat. *Female and Immature:* fine streaking on throat.
Size: 3³/₄ in.

Eastern Wood-Pewee

Contopus virens

The plaintive, whistled *pee-a-wee* of
the Eastern Wood-Pewee echoes sadly
through most woodlands in our area.
These mouse-colored summer residents are difficult to
sight until they loop out after a passing insect. A classic flycatcher, Eastern Wood-Pewees faithfully return to their preferred perch, at the mid-level in the forest, following each short
foraging flight.

The nest of the Eastern Wood-Pewee resembles nothing more than a
knot on a small limb, well camouflaged by both shape and color. The outer
walls of the structure are wallpapered with lichens, while the nest itself seems
too small for the bird sitting upon it. In addition to its concealing master-
piece, this small flycatcher vigorously defends its nest site against all intruders
who dare approach.

Similar Species: Willow Flycatcher (p. 81) has an eye ring and sings an
abrupt *fitz-bew* song. Acadian Flycatcher has a bold eye ring and a yellow
wash on its belly.

Quick I.D.: sparrow-sized; sexes similar; olive-
gray body; dark tail and wings; two faint wing
bars; no eye ring; dark upper mandible; pale
orange lower mandible.
Size: 6–6¹/₂ in.

Jan Feb Mar Apr May Jun Jul Aug Sept Oct Nov Dec

Willow Flycatcher
Empidonax traillii

Southern spring winds carry the first Willow Flycatchers into Illinois forests in mid- to late May. The day of their arrival is often easily recognized, because these small birds punctuate their presence with their simple and sneezy *fitz-bew* song. From swaying shrubby perches, Willow Flycatchers sing and survey their chosen territories.

The Willow Flycatcher is one of the boldest and most pugnacious songbirds in the open second-growth shrub forests of Illinois. During the nesting season, it is noisy and aggressive, driving away all avian intruders and fighting furiously with rival males. The confusing collection of empidonax flycatchers are the 'lords of the mosquitoes,' but the curse of the birdwatcher. The Willow, Least, Acadian and Alder flycatchers all pass through our area each year, and they are virtually indistinguishable in the field except by voice. Their confusing plumage, however, should not deter novice birders from the pleasantness of these small birds.

Similar Species: Eastern Wood-Pewee (p. 80) sings *pee-a-wee*. All other empidonax flycatchers have more pronounced eye rings and characteristic vocalizations: Acadian Flycatcher sings *peet seet*; Least Flycatcher sings *che bek*; Alder Flycatcher sings *fee-bee-o*.

Jan Feb Mar Apr May Jun Jul Aug Sept Oct Nov Dec

Quick I.D.: sparrow-sized; sexes similar; olive-brown upperparts; no eye ring; two white wing bars; long, narrow, dark tail; dark bill; light throat.
Size: 5–6 in.

Great Crested Flycatcher
Myiarchus crinitus

The Great Crested Flycatcher is most unusual in its selection of decor for its nest cavity: it occasionally lays a shed snakeskin as a door mat. This uncommon but noteworthy practice can identify the nest of this flycatcher, the only member of its family in Chicago to nest in a cavity. The objective of the Great Crested Flycatcher's infrequently seen nest decoration is not known, and these versatile birds have occasionally substituted plastic wrap for reptilian skin.

The Great Crested Flycatcher's name is somewhat misleading—this bird's crest can only truthfully be considered 'great' when compared to those of other flycatchers. Nevertheless, an objective opinion of this bird's name and behavior can be made after pleasant encounters along Chicago's lakefront parks or in woods along the Des Plaines River. Listen for it singing its distinctive *creep creep*.

Similar Species: Eastern Wood-Pewee (p. 80), Eastern Phoebe and other flycatchers are smaller and lack the lemon yellow belly and chestnut tail.

Quick I.D.: smaller than a robin; sexes similar; yellow belly; gray throat and head; dark olive-brown back and wings; chestnut tail lining; rufous wing linings; erect crest.
Size: 7–8 in.

Jan Feb Mar Apr May Jun Jul Aug Sept Oct Nov Dec

Eastern Kingbird
Tyrannus tyrannus

When one thinks of a tyrant, the image of a large, carnivorous dinosaur or a menacing ruler is much more likely to come to mind than that of a little bird. While the Eastern Kingbird may not initially seem to be as imposing as other known tyrants, this flycatcher certainly lives up to its scientific name, *Tyrannus tyrannus*. The Eastern Kingbird is pugnacious—it will fearlessly attack crows, hawks, other large birds and even humans who pass through its territory. The intruders are often vigorously pursued, pecked and plucked for some distance until the kingbird is satisfied that there is no further threat.

The courtship flight of the Eastern Kingbird, which can be seen occasionally in our area, is characterized by short, quivering wingbeats. It is a touching display, even for this little tyrant. The nest site is typically close to water, where the bird's next meal is only a sudden foraging flight away.

Similar Species: Tree Swallow (p. 86) and all other flycatchers lack the white terminal tail band and are not black and white.

Jan Feb Mar Apr May Jun Jul Aug Sept Oct Nov Dec

Quick I.D.: smaller than a robin; sexes similar; black head, back, wings and tail; white underparts; white terminal tail band; orange-red crown (rarely seen).
Size: 9 in.

Chimney Swift
Chaetura pelagica

The Chimney Swift is one of the frequent flyers of the bird world—only incubation keeps this bird off its wings—and it feeds, drinks, bathes and even mates in flight. During its four- to five-year average lifespan, these sailors of the air can travel more than one million miles. Swifts often forage for flying insects at great heights, and during the height of day they are visible only as specks in the distant sky. As the sun sinks to the horizon, however, flocks of Chimney Swifts can be seen spiraling into their evening roosts.

Swifts are shaped much like swallows—long, tapering wings, a small bill, a wide gape and a long, sleek body—but they share no close relationship. The wingbeat of swifts looks uncomfortable, but it doesn't hamper the graceful flight of these aerial masters, which cast a distinct boomerang silhouette when they glide. Swifts, when not in flight, use their small but strong claws to cling precariously to vertical surfaces. Because many old, hollow hardwood trees have been removed from our area since colonization, Chimney Swifts have adopted human structures, such as inactive chimneys, as common nesting sites.

Similar Species: All swallows have a smooth, direct flight style and broader wings.

Quick I.D.: smaller than a sparrow; sexes similar; boomerang flight profile; brown overall; slim.
Size: 5¹/₂ in.

Jan Feb Mar Apr May Jun Jul Aug Sept Oct Nov Dec

Purple Martin
Progne subis

Late summer is a very busy time around a Purple Martin complex. Adults spiral around the large, communal next box, coming and going from foraging forays. The year's young perch at the opening of their apartment cavity, impatiently waiting for their parents to return with a mouthful of flying insects. A patient observer watching the colonies at the Chicago Botanic Garden will notice how orderly the apparent confusion is to the martin, and how efficiently the crowded complex is negotiated.

These fascinating experiences are rewards to residents who erect Purple Martin complexes, which should be high on a pole in the middle of a large, open area often near a large waterbody. The complex should be cleaned and plugged up once the birds have left, until they return in spring. House Sparrows and European Starlings will overthrow the preferred tenant if given a chance.

Similar Species: Barn Swallow (p. 88) has a deeply forked tail. Tree Swallow (p. 86) has a white belly. European Starling (p. 117) has a long bill and a short tail.

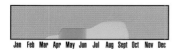

Quick I.D.: smaller than a robin; pointed wings; forked tail; small bill. *Male:* deep, glossy blue plumage. *Female* and *Immature:* gray underparts; duller backs.
Size: 7–8 in.

Tree Swallow
Tachycineta bicolor

Depending on food availability, Tree Swallows forage over great distances, darting above open fields and wetlands as they catch flying insects in their bills. These bicolored birds occasionally swoop down to the water's surface for a quick drink and bath. In bad weather, Tree Swallows might fly up to five miles to distant marshes or lakes to find flying insects.

The Tree Swallow is among the first migrants to arrive in the Chicago area, often beating the onset of spring weather. It returns to our freshwater marshes by late March to begin its reproductive cycle. It nests in abandoned woodpecker cavities and in nest boxes intended primarily for bluebirds. The cavity is lined with weeds, grasses and long feathers. When the parents leave the nest for long periods of time, they cover the eggs with feathers. The females lay and incubate four to six eggs for up to 16 days. Once the birds hatch, the young leave the cavity within three weeks to begin their aerial lives.

Similar Species: Chimney Swift (p. 84) has slimmer wings and a darker belly. Bank Swallow (p. 87) and Northern Rough-winged Swallow both lack the blue upperparts.

Quick I.D.: sparrow-sized; sexes similar; iridescent blue plumage; white underparts; dark rump; small bill and feet. *In flight:* long, pointed wings; shallowly forked tail.
Size: 5–6 in.

Jan Feb Mar Apr May Jun Jul Aug Sept Oct Nov Dec

Bank Swallow
Riparia riparia

Bank Swallows cruise over wetlands, fields and meadows at low altitudes, gracefully catching flying insects in flight. They often catch transforming insects just as they are emerging from the water to enter their adult stage.

Bank Swallows begin nesting in April. As their name suggests, they choose dirt banks, such as those found in gravel pits and at Waukegan Beach, in which to build their nest cavity. These small birds diligently excavate the burrow, first with their small bill and later with their feet. Incredibly, Bank Swallows have been known to kick and scratch out a burrow five feet long, but the typical length is two to three feet. An active Bank Swallow colony is difficult to approach undetected, because the frightened birds launch themselves from their burrows and circle overhead until the threat passes.

Similar Species: Tree Swallow (p. 86) has blue upperparts.
Northern Rough-winged Swallow lacks the dark chest band.

Quick I.D.: sparrow-sized; sexes similar; brown upperparts; light underparts; dark band on chest; long, pointed wings; small bill; dark cheek; dark rump; small legs.
Size: 5–6 in.

Jan Feb Mar Apr May Jun Jul Aug Sept Oct Nov Dec

Barn Swallow
Hirundo rustica

The graceful flight of the Barn Swallow is a common summer sight. It often forages at low altitudes, so its deeply forked tail is easily observed. The Barn Swallow is actually the only swallow in Chicago to have a 'swallow-tail.' The name 'swallow' originated in Europe, where the Barn Swallow is also common, and where it is simply called the Swallow.

The Barn Swallow builds its cup-shaped mud nests in the eaves of barns, bridges and picnic shelters, or in any other structure that provides protection from the rain. Because the Barn Swallow is often closely associated with human structures, it is not uncommon for a nervous parent bird to dive repeatedly at human 'intruders,' encouraging them to retreat.

Similar Species: Purple Martin (p. 85) has a shorter tail and lacks the russet throat and forehead.

Quick I.D.: larger than a sparrow; sexes similar, but female is a bit duller; deeply forked tail; glossy blue back, wings and tail; chestnut underparts; russet throat and forehead.
Size: 6–8 in.

Jan Feb Mar Apr May Jun Jul Aug Sept Oct Nov Dec

Blue Jay
Cyanocitta cristata

The Blue Jay is one of our region's most identifiable birds. With its loud *jay-jay-jay* call, blue-and-white plumage and large crest, it is familiar to anyone with sunflower seeds or peanuts at their birdfeeder. Blue Jays are intelligent, aggressive and adaptable birds that don't hesitate to drive smaller birds, squirrels or even cats away when they feel threatened. Although present year-round, Blue Jays seem more numerous and noticeable throughout our winter months.

The Blue Jay represents all the admirable virtues and aggressive qualities of the corvid family. While it is beautiful, resourceful and vocally diverse, the Blue Jay can be one of the most annoying and mischievous birds, and no predator is too formidable for this bird to harass. With noisy calls, Blue Jays wake up neighborhoods and forests where they are the self-appointed guardians, but this colorful bird's extroverted character and boldness outweigh its occasional briefly annoying behavior.

Similar Species: None.

Jan Feb Mar Apr May Jun Jul Aug Sept Oct Nov Dec

Quick I.D.: larger than a robin; sexes similar; blue crest, back, wings and tail; black 'necklace'; white wing bars; light belly.
Size: 11–12 in.

American Crow

Corvus brachyrhynchos

The American Crow calls with a classic, long, descending *caaaw*. In late summer and fall, when their reproductive duties are completed, crows group together to roost in flocks, known as a 'murders.' The crow population has exploded in our area in recent years, and large flocks can be seen almost anywhere in and around Chicago.

This large, black bird's intelligence has led it into many confrontations with humans, from which it often emerges the victor. Scientific studies have shown that crows are capable of solving simple problems, which comes as no surprise to anyone who has watched crows snip open garbage bags with scissors-like precision.

Similar Species: None.

Quick I.D.: small gull–sized; sexes similar; all black; fan-shaped tail; slim overall.
Size: 18–20 in.

Jan Feb Mar Apr May Jun Jul Aug Sept Oct Nov Dec

Black-capped Chickadee

Poecile atricapillus

The Black-capped Chickadee is one of the most pleasant birds in urban and forested areas, often seeming to greet walkers along trails. It is a common sight in Chicago and can be found in every wooded area in parks and in most landscaped backyards. Throughout most of the year, chickadees move about in loose flocks, investigating nooks and crannies for food and uttering their delicate *chick-a-dee-dee-dee* calls.

During spring, Black-capped Chickadees seem strangely absent from city parks and wooded ravines, because they remain inconspicuous while nesting. Once the first fall chill arrives, the woods are once again vibrant with their busy activities.

Similar Species: White-breasted Nuthatch (p. 92) lacks a black chin and has a short tail and red undertail coverts. Tufted Titmouse lacks a black cap and bib. Blackpoll Warbler is a migrant that has orange legs and streaked underparts.

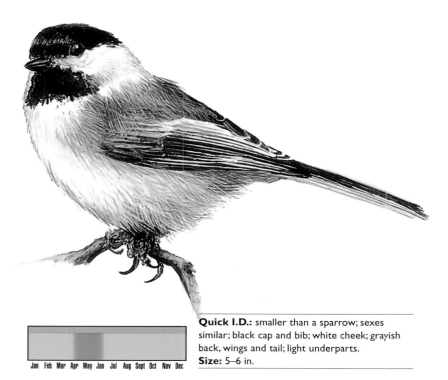

Jan Feb Mar Apr May Jun Jul Aug Sept Oct Nov Dec

Quick I.D.: smaller than a sparrow; sexes similar; black cap and bib; white cheek; grayish back, wings and tail; light underparts.

Size: 5–6 in.

White-breasted Nuthatch
Sitta carolinensis

To the novice birdwatcher, seeing a White-breasted Nuthatch call repeatedly while clinging to the underside of a branch is an odd sight. To nuthatches, however, this gravity-defying act is as natural as flight is to other birds. A nuthatch will frequently pause in mid-descent, arch its head out at right angles to the trunk and give its distinctive and often repeated *yarnk-yarnk-yarnk* call. It makes its seemingly dangerous headfirst hops seem routine.

White-breasted Nuthatches frequently visit backyard feeders. Nuthatches seem less at home on the level platform feeders, where they cast aside their tree-trunk talent for a cautious meal of sunflower seeds.

Similar Species: Black-capped Chickadee (p. 91) has a black bib and a longer tail. Red-breasted Nuthatch has a red breast and a black eye line.

Quick I.D.: sparrow-sized. *Male:* black cap; white cheek and breast; steel blue back, wings and tail; straight bill; short tail; russet undertail coverts. *Female:* similar but with a grayish cap.
Size: 6 in.

Jan Feb Mar Apr May Jun Jul Aug Sept Oct Nov Dec

House Wren
Troglodytes aedon

This common bird of backyards, city parks and woodlands sings as though its lungs were bottomless. The sweet, warbling song of the House Wren is distinguished by its melodious tone and its uninterrupted endurance. Although the House Wren is far smaller than a sparrow, it offers an unending song in one breath.

Like all wrens, the House Wren frequently carries its short tail cocked straight up. This bird is often observed from May to September skulking beneath the dense understory. House Wrens seem particularly fond of shrubby bottom woods, where they nest in tree cavities or near bluebird boxes. As spring arrives, the House Wren treats Chicago neighborhoods to a few weeks of wonderful warbles, and then it channels its energy to the task of reproduction.

Similar Species: Winter Wren has cinnamon plumage and its tail is shorter than its legs. Carolina Wren has white eyebrows.

Jan Feb Mar Apr May Jun Jul Aug Sept Oct Nov Dec

Quick I.D.: smaller than a sparrow; sexes similar; brown overall; tail is often cocked up; bill is slightly downcurved; tail is as long as legs.
Size: 5 in.

Marsh Wren
Cistothorus palustris

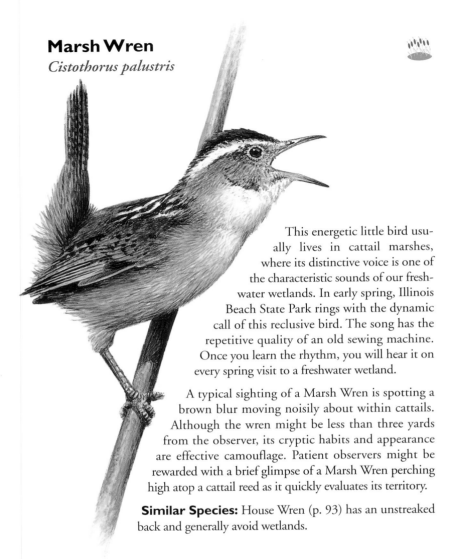

This energetic little bird usually lives in cattail marshes, where its distinctive voice is one of the characteristic sounds of our freshwater wetlands. In early spring, Illinois Beach State Park rings with the dynamic call of this reclusive bird. The song has the repetitive quality of an old sewing machine. Once you learn the rhythm, you will hear it on every spring visit to a freshwater wetland.

A typical sighting of a Marsh Wren is spotting a brown blur moving noisily about within cattails. Although the wren might be less than three yards from the observer, its cryptic habits and appearance are effective camouflage. Patient observers might be rewarded with a brief glimpse of a Marsh Wren perching high atop a cattail reed as it quickly evaluates its territory.

Similar Species: House Wren (p. 93) has an unstreaked back and generally avoid wetlands.

Quick I.D.: smaller than a sparrow; sexes similar; brown overall; white streaking on back; white eye line; light throat and breast; cocked-up tail.
Size: 4–5¹/₂ in.

Jan Feb Mar Apr May Jun Jul Aug Sept Oct Nov Dec

Golden-crowned Kinglet
Regulus satrapa

The high-pitched, tinkling voice of the Golden-crowned Kinglet is as familiar as the sweet smell of pine and fir in coniferous forests. Although not immediately obvious to the uninformed passerby, a birdwatcher with a keen ear, patience and the willingness to draw down this smallest of North American songbirds with squeaks and pishes will encounter kinglets on many outdoor trips. During late fall, early winter and early spring, tall conifers in Chicago's parks and older communities come alive with the sound of the Golden-crowned Kinglet's faint, high-pitched, accelerating *tsee-tsee-tsee-tsee, why do you shilly-shally?*

As these tiny birds descend in loose flocks around a curious onlooker, their indistinct plumage and voice offer little excitement. It is when the flock circles nearby, using the branches as swings and trapezes, flashing their regal crowns, that the magic of the kinglet emerges.

Similar Species: Ruby-crowned Kinglet (p. 96) lacks the black outline to the crown.

Jan Feb Mar Apr May Jun Jul Aug Sept Oct Nov Dec

Quick I.D.: smaller than a sparrow; plump; dark olive; white wing bars; dark tail and wings; white eyebrows. *Male:* fiery orange crown bordered by yellow and black. *Female:* lemon yellow crown bordered by black.
Size: 4 in.

Ruby-crowned Kinglet
Regulus calendula

These kinglets are visitors to Chicago parks and backyards, especially among coniferous trees. Kinglets always appear nervous, with their tails and wings flicking continuously as they hop from branch to branch in search of grubs and insect eggs.

The Ruby-crowned Kinglet is similar to the Golden-crowned Kinglet in size, habits and coloration, but it has a hidden ruby crown. 'Rubies' are heard more often then they are seen, and they produce an amazing amount of noise for birds of their size. Their distinctive song starts like a motor chugging to life, and then the kinglets fire off a series of loud, rising *chewy-chewy-chewy-chewys*. These final excitable phrases are often the only recognizable part of the song.

Similar Species: Golden-crowned Kinglet (p. 95) has a black outline to the crown.

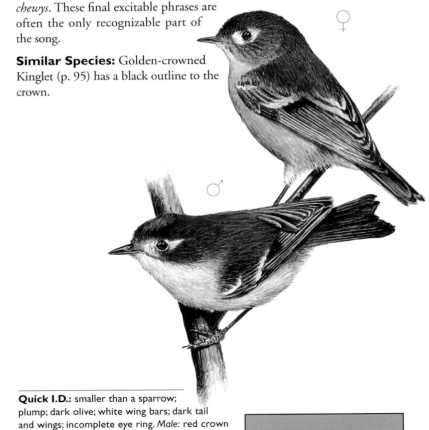

Quick I.D.: smaller than a sparrow; plump; dark olive; white wing bars; dark tail and wings; incomplete eye ring. *Male:* red crown (infrequently seen). *Female:* no red crown.
Size: 4 in.

Jan Feb Mar Apr May Jun Jul Aug Sept Oct Nov Dec

Blue-gray Gnatcatcher
Polioptila caerulea

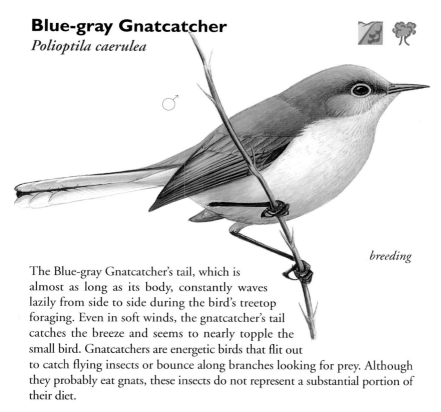

♂

breeding

The Blue-gray Gnatcatcher's tail, which is almost as long as its body, constantly waves lazily from side to side during the bird's treetop foraging. Even in soft winds, the gnatcatcher's tail catches the breeze and seems to nearly topple the small bird. Gnatcatchers are energetic birds that flit out to catch flying insects or bounce along branches looking for prey. Although they probably eat gnats, these insects do not represent a substantial portion of their diet.

Blue-gray Gnatcatchers build their small nests at mid-height in a deciduous tree, often in riparian river courses. Both sexes build the structure and cleverly conceal its identity by plastering the outside with lichens and spider silk. Females lay four or five small eggs, and often attempt a second brood during July. These small birds are expanding their range and becoming increasingly common throughout our area, creating a wondrous diversion to attentive eyes that drift to our treetops.

Similar Species: Ruby-crowned Kinglet (p. 96) and Golden-crowned Kinglet (p. 95) are olive-green overall, with short tails and wing bars. Gray Catbird (p. 118) is much larger and has russet undertail coverts.

Jan Feb Mar Apr May Jun Jul Aug Sept Oct Nov Dec

Quick I.D.: smaller than a sparrow; long tail; white eye ring; pale gray underparts; no wing bars; tail is black above with white outer tail feathers. *Breeding male:* dark blue-gray upperparts; black-bordered crown. *Female:* light gray upperparts.
Size: 4^1/$_2$–5 in.

Eastern Bluebird

Sialia sialis

Dressed with the colors of the cool sky on its back and the warm setting sun on its chest, the male Eastern Bluebird looks like a piece of pure sky come to life. To fully appreciate this specialty, try to spot a male as he sets up his territory on a crisp, early spring morning in open country, such as at Illinois Beach State Park or Ryerson Woods.

The Eastern Bluebird lost many of its natural nesting sites in vacant cavities to House Sparrows and European Starlings and to the removal of dead trees from much of our area. Concerned residents rallied for this bird, however, and put up hundreds of nesting boxes to compensate for the losses. The Eastern Bluebird population has slowly increased as a result, and the vigilant residents have been rewarded with the sight of the bird's beautiful plumage in the Midwest's landscape.

Similar Species: American Robin (p. 101) has a dark back and lacks any blue. Male Indigo Bunting (p. 141) lacks the red breast and has a conical bill.

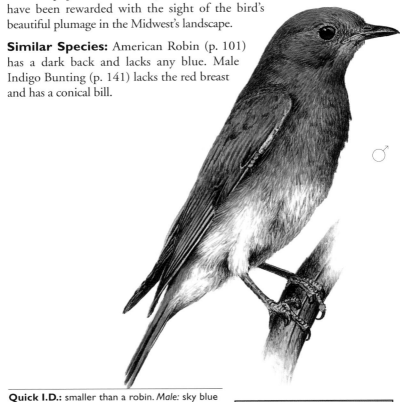

♂

Quick I.D.: smaller than a robin. *Male:* sky blue back; rusty throat and breast; white undertail coverts; thin bill. *Female:* less intense blue.
Size: 6–7 in.

Jan Feb Mar Apr May Jun Jul Aug Sept Oct Nov Dec

Veery
Catharus fuscescens

Like a tumbling waterfall, the Veery's voice descends with a liquid ripple. This bird, like all other thrushes, is a master of melodies and offers its unequaled songs to forests gradually darkening with the setting sun. The Veery is one of the last singers in the evening, and if you turn your ear to woodlands along the Des Plaines River or at Volo Bog during the last weeks of May, you'll have an audio treat.

The Veery is perhaps the most terrestrial of Chicago's thrushes; it frequently nests on the ground. In characteristic thrush style, the Veery searches for grubs and caterpillars by shuffling through loose leaf litter. When an invertebrate delicacy is found, it is swallowed quickly, and the ever-vigilant Veery cautiously looks about before renewing the hunt.

Similar Species: Wood (p. 100), Hermit and Swainson's thrushes are more boldly patterned on the breast, and each has a characteristic song.

Jan Feb Mar Apr May Jun Jul Aug Sept Oct Nov Dec

Quick I.D.: smaller than a robin; sexes similar; reddish-brown head, back, rump and tail; faint spotting on throat; no conspicuous eye ring.
Size: 7–8 in.

Wood Thrush
Hylocichla mustelina

The Wood Thrush's musical warble—*Will you live with me? Way up high in a tree, I'll come right down and ... seeee*—has faded from many Illinois woodlands. The Wood Thrush was once the voice of our hardwood forests, but this species has declined because of forest fragmentation. Broken forests invite common predators, such as the skunk, fox, crow and jay, which traditionally had no access to Wood Thrush nests deep within the protected confines of vast hardwoods. Cowbirds, historically linked to the open fields, now parasitize this thrush's nests, depositing foreign eggs within its brood.

Like the hope and faith that seem to flow with the Wood Thrush's melody, the future might still hold promise for this often-glorified songbird. As pioneer farms are slowly abandoned and we learn to value the sanctity of a bird song, the wild spirit of the Wood Thrush offers up an optimistic note.

Similar Species: Veery (p. 99), Hermit Thrush and Swainson's Thrush all lack the bold black chest spots and reddish head.

Quick I.D.: smaller than a robin; sexes similar; plump; large, black spots on white breast; reddish-brown head; brown rump and tail; white eye ring.
Size: 7¹/₂–8¹/₂ in.

Jan Feb Mar Apr May Jun Jul Aug Sept Oct Nov Dec

American Robin

Turdus migratorius

If not for its abundance, the American Robin's voice and plumage would inspire pause and praise from casual onlookers. However, acclimatization has dealt the robin an unfair hand, and it is generally not fully appreciated for the pleasures it offers the eyes and ears of Chicago-area residents.

Nevertheless, the American Robin's close relationship with urban areas has allowed many residents an insight into a bird's life. A robin dashing around a yard in search of worms or ripe berries is as familiar to many people as its early pre-dawn, three-part *cheerily-cheery up-cheerio* song. American Robins also make up part of the emotional landscape of communities as their cheery song, their spotted young and occasionally even their deaths are experiences shared by their human neighbors.

American Robins are year-round residents in Chicago, but the bird dashing on your lawn in June might not be the same bird that shivers in February. Unnoticed by most residents, the neighborhood robins take seasonal shifts; new birds arrive from the north just when some summer residents depart for southern climes in fall.

Similar Species: Immature robins can be confused with other thrushes, but robins always have at least a hint of red in the breast.

Quick I.D.: smaller than a jay; dark head, back and tail; yellow bill; striped throat; white undertail coverts. *Male:* brick red breast; darker hood. *Female:* slightly more orange breast; lighter hood. **Size:** 9–11 in.

Jan Feb Mar Apr May Jun Jul Aug Sept Oct Nov Dec

Warbling Vireo
Vireo gilvus

The Warbling Vireo can be quite common during the summer months, but you still need to make a prolonged search before spotting this bird. Lacking any splashy field marks, the Warbling Vireo is exceedingly difficult to spot unless it moves. Searching the treetops for this inconspicuous bird may be a 'pain in the neck,' but the satisfaction in visually confirming its identity can be rewarding.

The velvety voice of the Warbling Vireo contrasts sharply with its dull, nondescript plumage. The often-repeated *I love you, I love you, I love you Ma'am* song delights the listening forest with its oscillating quality. The phrases finish on an upbeat, as if the bird is asking a question of the wilds.

Similar Species: Red-eyed Vireo (p. 103) has a black-and-white eyebrow and a gray cap.

breeding

Quick I.D.: smaller than a sparrow; sexes similar; indistinct white eyebrow; no wing bars; olive-gray upperparts; greenish flanks; light underparts; gray crown.
Size: 4¹/₂–5¹/₂ in.

Jan Feb Mar Apr May Jun Jul Aug Sept Oct Nov Dec

Red-eyed Vireo
Vireo olivaceus

breeding

The Red-eyed Vireo is the undisputed champion of singing endurance. During the breeding season, males sing from tall deciduous trees throughout the day. Most songbirds stop their courting melodies five or six hours after sunrise, but the Red-eyed Vireo seems to gain momentum as the day progresses. One patient ornithologist estimated that the energetic Red-eyed Vireo sings its memorable phrase—*look up, way up, tree top, see me, here-I-am*—10,000 to 20,000 times a day.

Visual identification of the Red-eyed Vireo is much harder, because its olive-brown color conceals it well among the foliage of deciduous trees. Although this vireo does indeed have red eyes, this feature can only be seen through powerful binoculars in excellent light conditions.

Similar Species: Warbling Vireo (p. 102) is larger and lacks the black-and-white eyebrow.

Jan Feb Mar Apr May Jun Jul Aug Sept Oct Nov Dec

Quick I.D.: sparrow-sized; sexes similar; gray crown bordered by black; white eyebrow; green back; white underparts; red eyes.
Size: 6 in.

Blue-winged Warbler

Vermivora pinus

There is nothing sinister to the thin, slick black eye line of this dainty little warbler; rather, its head gear adds an unusual high-tech style to this summer resident. This golden-bodied songbird has a song that is equally distinctive—its buzzy bellow ascends and then abruptly descends, like an inhaled-exhaled *bee-buzz*. These qualities can be experienced in May and June, during short walks around Ryerson Conservation Area, Cuba Marsh and Swallow Cliffs woods.

Blue-winged Warblers have also gained fame for their habit of breeding with other species. One of the few common examples of hybrids occur when this warbler interbreeds with the Golden-winged Warbler, producing the 'Brewster's Warbler.' This hybrid is found rarely in the Chicago area, and it occurs in far lesser numbers than its Blue-winged forebear.

Similar Species: Yellow Warbler (p. 106) lacks the black eye line and blue-gray wings. Golden-winged Warbler has a dark throat and white underparts. 'Brewster's Warbler' lacks the blue-gray wings and doesn't have as pure yellow underparts.

Quick I.D.: smaller than a sparrow; yellow body; black mask; blue-gray wings and tail; two merged white wing bars; dark legs. *Male:* brighter yellow on crown and nape. *Female:* yellow-green on head and nape; duller overall.
Size: 4–4¹/₂ in.

Jan Feb Mar Apr May Jun Jul Aug Sept Oct Nov Dec

Nashville Warbler

Vermivora ruficapilla

This common warbler has an identity crisis, not so much a result of its unassuming attire but because of its misleading name. If this small bird's name must reflect a place name, then the natural choice should be the 'Midwest Warbler.' A large part of this species's American breeding range is just to the north of us in Wisconsin, so its present name simply does not describe a location where it can be commonly found. The name seemed appropriate to Alexander Wilson when he collected the first specimen in Tennessee, but that bird was only passing through.

Such a misnomer is not an isolated incident, and many other warblers in Illinois bear the names given to them during migration. The Cape May (named for a site in New Jersey), Tennessee, Palm and Magnolia warblers are all northern-nesting species, but they bear names that do not reflect their breeding habits.

Nashville Warblers can be easily found fairly low in the flowering 'crabs' and hawthorns in our city parks and forest preserves.

Similar Species: Common Yellowthroat (p. 114) has a black mask. Connecticut Warbler is larger.

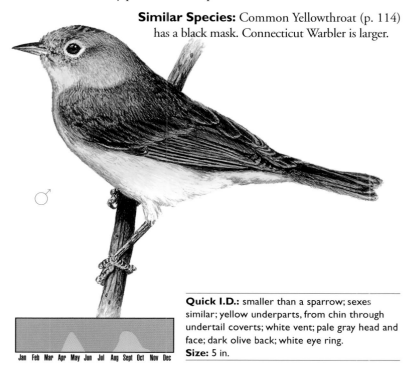

Jan Feb Mar Apr May Jun Jul Aug Sept Oct Nov Dec

Quick I.D.: smaller than a sparrow; sexes similar; yellow underparts, from chin through undertail coverts; white vent; pale gray head and face; dark olive back; white eye ring.
Size: 5 in.

Yellow Warbler
Dendroica petechia

The Yellow Warbler is common in shrublands and in groves of alder, willow and cottonwood. As a consequence of its abundance, it is usually the first warbler birdwatchers identify in their lives, and every year thereafter. From mid-May through August, this brilliantly colored warbler is easily found in appropriate habitat throughout our area.

During our winters, Yellow Warblers migrate to the tropics, spending September to April in Mexico and South America. Following the first warm days of spring, the first of the Yellow Warblers return. Their distinctive courtship song—*sweet-sweet-sweet I'm so-so sweet*—is easily recognized in early May despite its eight-month absence. In true warbler fashion, the summertime activities of the Yellow Warbler are energetic and inquisitive, flitting from branch to branch in search of juicy caterpillars, aphids and beetles.

Similar Species: Wilson's Warbler has a small, black cap.

Quick I.D.: smaller than a sparrow; yellow overall; darker back, wings and tail; dark eyes and bill. *Male:* fine red streaking on breast. *Female:* no red streaking.
Size: 4–5 in.

Jan Feb Mar Apr May Jun Jul Aug Sept Oct Nov Dec

Chestnut-sided Warbler
Dendroica pensylvanica

♂

breeding

Dropping down to human eye-level, the curious Chestnut-sided Warbler invites all into young deciduous stands with a hearty *so pleased pleased pleased to meet-cha* greeting. This woodland migrant appears genuinely hospitable, and in its flitty behavior it often passes within one branch of onlookers. Its distinctive chestnut-and-white belly accentuates the male warbler's timeless style for springtime fashion.

Chestnut-sided Warblers can be among the most common warblers in Chicago but only for a few weeks in spring and fall. Young, re-growing forests were far less common before colonization than they are today. Because of this change, it is now possible to see more Chestnut-sided Warblers in a single day during migration than some of the great pioneering naturalists saw in their entire lives.

Similar Species: Bay-breasted Warbler lacks the yellow crown and the white cheek and throat. Cape May Warbler lacks the white underparts.

Jan Feb Mar Apr May Jun Jul Aug Sept Oct Nov Dec

Quick I.D.: smaller than a sparrow. *Breeding male:* white underparts; chestnut flanks; yellow crown; white cheek; light yellow wing bars; black and green–streaked back. *Breeding female:* less brilliant markings and colors.
Size: 5 in.

Yellow-rumped Warbler
Dendroica coronata

breeding

This spirited songbird is as common as it is delightful. Its contrasting colors, curiosity and tinkling trill are enthusiastically admired by even the most jaded birdwatcher. Yellow-rumped Warblers are the only year-round warbler in the Chicago area, with a few hardy individuals remaining to feed on poison ivy, juniper and hawthorn berries. However, it is not during the coldest months that Yellow-rumps are most noticeable; rather it is during late April and early May, when trees along the lakefront and forest preserves with water courses come alive with these colorful birds.

Most experienced birdwatchers continue to call these birds 'Myrtle Warblers.' Until fairly recently, our white-throated form was considered distinct from the western, yellow-throated form, the 'Audubon's Warbler.' This, however, has changed, resulting in the combined name of the Yellow-rumped Warbler.

Similar Species: Magnolia Warbler has yellow underparts and white patches in the tail.

Quick I.D.: smaller than a sparrow; blue-black back, tail and wings; yellow rump, crown and shoulder patches; white throat; faint white wing bars; dark chest band; white belly; dark cheek. *Male:* bright colors. *Female:* less intense colors.
Size: 5–6 in.

Jan Feb Mar Apr May Jun Jul Aug Sept Oct Nov Dec

Palm Warbler
Dendroica palmarum

For a few days each spring, large numbers of Palm Warblers pass through our area on route to their northern breeding grounds. Palm Warblers are lively transients; they can generally be found low in shrubs or hopping along trails and forest clearings gleaning for grasshoppers, beetles, moths and flies as comfortably as any sparrow. Their foraging behavior is surprisingly unique among the wood warblers, which as a group generally go about their foraging in trees and shrubs.

The Palm Warbler's yellow underparts gleam surprisingly in sunlight, while the dull red cap strikes a dark contrast. This warbler's most distinctive trait is perhaps its incessant habit of wagging its tail, regardless of whether it is perched or hopping along on the ground. Perhaps it should have been named for this wagging feature, because it is rarely seen among palms, even on its tropical wintering grounds.

Similar Species: Yellow-rumped Warbler (p. 108) has a yellow rump, darker upperparts and white wing bars. Chipping Sparrow (p. 123) has a stouter body, unstreaked underparts and no yellow in the plumage.

breeding

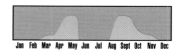

Jan Feb Mar Apr May Jun Jul Aug Sept Oct Nov Dec

Quick I.D.: sparrow-sized; sexes similar; chestnut cap; yellow throat and undertail coverts; streaked brown breast and belly; whitish-yellow eyebrow; olive-brown upperparts.
Size: 5¹/₂ in.

Black-and-white Warbler

Mniotilta varia

In general appearance, the Black-and-white Warbler seems quite normal, but its foraging behavior lies in sharp contrast to most of its warbler kin. Rather than dancing quickly between twig perches like most warblers, Black-and-white Warblers have a foraging strategy similar to an entirely unrelated group of birds—the nuthatches. As if possessed by nuthatch envy, Black-and-white Warblers hop gingerly up and down tree trunks in search of insect eggs, larval insects, beetles, spiders and other invertebrates.

Unfortunately, forest fragmentation and development in the Chicago area have forced breeding birds elsewhere. They do occur regularly throughout our area in migration, appearing in backyards and forest preserves and in Lincoln Park during their prolonged spring and fall passages. A novice birdwatcher can easily identify this two-toned and oddly behaved warbler. A keen ear also helps: the gentle oscillating song—like a wheel in need of greasing—is easily identified and remembered.

Similar Species: Blackpoll Warbler has orange legs and a solid black cap.

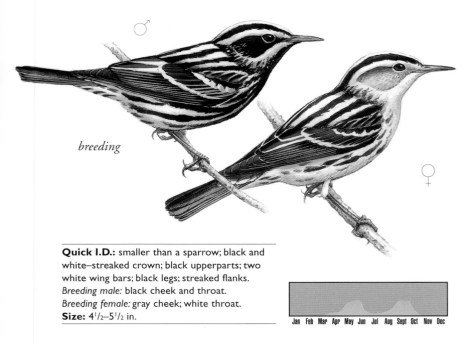

breeding

Quick I.D.: smaller than a sparrow; black and white–streaked crown; black upperparts; two white wing bars; black legs; streaked flanks.
Breeding male: black cheek and throat.
Breeding female: gray cheek; white throat.
Size: 4¹/₂–5¹/₂ in.

Jan Feb Mar Apr May Jun Jul Aug Sept Oct Nov Dec

American Redstart
Setophaga ruticilla

Like an over-energized wind-up toy, the American Redstart flits from branch to branch in a dizzying pursuit of prey. Never for a moment will a redstart pause; even while it's perched, its orange-splashed tail waves gently behind. This erratic and amusing behavior is easily observed in the bird's summering ground as well as its Central American wintering habitat, where it is affectionately known as *candelita* (the little candle). With constantly quivering wings, tail and shoulders, the redstart's patches are sparks of life in any dark forest.

Although American Redstarts breed sparingly in the Chicago area, their songs are so wonderfully various that even after a spring season is spent listening to them, their songs can still be confusing. While walking in any forest area in May, and in Ryerson Conservation Area, Swallow Cliff woods and Chain O'Lakes State Park in summer, you can discover the bird's energy and enthusiasm.

Similar Species: Red-winged Blackbird (p. 132) is much larger and has no red on its chest or tail.

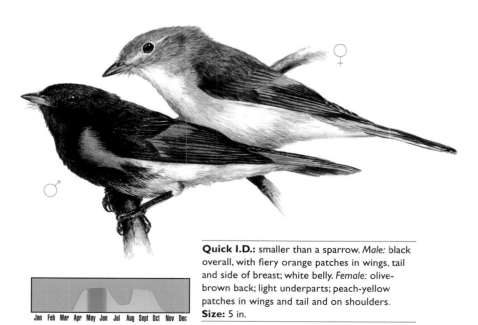

Jan Feb Mar Apr May Jun Jul Aug Sept Oct Nov Dec

Quick I.D.: smaller than a sparrow. *Male:* black overall, with fiery orange patches in wings, tail and side of breast; white belly. *Female:* olive-brown back; light underparts; peach-yellow patches in wings and tail and on shoulders. **Size:** 5 in.

Ovenbird
Seiurus aurocapillus

The Ovenbird—or at least its song *teacher teacher Teacher TEACHER*—is a trademark of this bird's breeding habitat. Its loud and distinctive song announces its presence in deciduous woods, and its noisy habit of walking through the undergrowth nearly reveals its precise location. Despite having a good indication of the Ovenbird's location, this songbird's cryptic plumage and its stubborn refusal to become airborne frustrate many birders intent on a quick peek. Rarely will Ovenbirds expose themselves to the open forest; they seem most comfortable in the tangle of shrubs, stumps and dead leaves.

The sharp, loud call of the Ovenbird rises from the dense layer of shrubs and plants and is one of the most distinctive voices of Chicago-area forests. Unfortunately, our disappearing forests have also taken a toll on this special bird, because it continually yields forest patches in the face of development.

Similar Species: Wood Thrush (p. 100) is much larger and lacks the streaked russet-orange crown. Northern Waterthrush (p. 113) lacks the russet-orange crown stripe and has a light eyebrow.

Quick I.D.: sparrow-sized; sexes similar; heavily streaked breast; olive-brown back; russet-orange crown stripe bordered by black; pinkish legs.
Size: 6 in.

Jan Feb Mar Apr May Jun Jul Aug Sept Oct Nov Dec

Northern Waterthrush
Seiurus noveboracensis

The Northern Waterthrush is not much of a visual bird but rather a testament song of wet woods. Northern Waterthrushes are well recognized and admired through song—a loud staccato *chew chew chew chew where-where-where-where-where*—the quality of which seems perfectly suited to their inhospitable haunts. It, perhaps better than any other bird of the Chicago area, raises the need for aspiring bird lovers to learn the calls and songs of these creatures.

A first glimpse of this unusual warbler in its wet woodland haunts reminds birdwatchers of a Spotted Sandpiper. The teetering body and heavily spotted Northern Waterthrush bobbing around a puddle can be accidentally mistaken for these quite different birds. The Northern Waterthrush is a rather common migrant along the shorelines of Lake Michigan and along rivers in forest preserves, where these birds are often encountered in May and September.

Similar Species: Ovenbird (p. 112) lacks the eyebrow and has an eye ring. Louisiana Waterthrush has a whiter eyebrow extending to the nape and an unstreaked throat.

Jan Feb Mar Apr May Jun Jul Aug Sept Oct Nov Dec

Quick I.D.: sparrow-sized; sexes similar; solid brown upperparts; light, heavily streaked, yellowish underparts; yellowish eyebrow; dark eye line; streaked cheek; light-colored legs. **Size:** 5¹/₂–6 in.

Common Yellowthroat
Geothlypis trichas

With so much diversity in North America's wood warbler clan, it is no surprise that one species has forsaken forests in favor of cattail marshes. The male Common Yellowthroat is easily identified by his black mask or by his oscillating *witchety-witchety-witchety* song. In our area, this energetic warbler reaches its highest abundance along wetland brambles and cattails, but it can be seen and heard along the vegetation bordering many freshwater marshes.

Female yellowthroats are rarely seen because they keep to their nests, deep within the thick vegetation surrounding marshes. The Common Yellowthroat's nests are often parasitized by Brown-headed Cowbirds. Should the nest avoid these common nest parasites, three to five young hatch after only about 12 days of incubation. These young continue their rapid development, soon leaving the nest and allowing the parents to repeat the process once again.

Similar Species: Male is distinct. Female Nashville Warbler (p. 105) has dark brown legs and an eye ring.

Quick I.D.: smaller than a sparrow; pinkish legs; yellow throat and underparts; olive upperparts. *Male:* black mask; white border on forehead. *Female:* no mask.
Size: 4¹/₂–5¹/₂ in.

Jan Feb Mar Apr May Jun Jul Aug Sept Oct Nov Dec

Scarlet Tanager
Piranga olivacea

breeding

♂

The tropical appearance of the Scarlet Tanager's plumage reinforces the link between the forests of South America and eastern North America. A winter resident of the tropics and a breeder in Chicago's mixed-woods, this tanager is vulnerable to deforestation at both extremes of its range.

Scarlet Tanagers can be difficult to see despite their tropical wardrobe, because they tend to sing their throaty, robin-like warble—*hurry-worry-lurry-scurry*—from high up in deciduous forest canopies. Because its song has the same quality as a robin's song, the tanager is frequently disregarded as a common woodland voice. Novice birdwatchers should listen for its hiccup-like *chick-burr* call as it cascades to the forest floor.

The Scarlet Tanager is one of Chicago's most breathtaking birds, and every brief encounter is sure to make you wish that the meeting might have lasted just a little longer.

Similar Species: Northern Cardinal (p. 139), Baltimore Oriole (p. 136) and Orchard Oriole lack the combination of an all-red body and black wings.

Jan Feb Mar Apr May Jun Jul Aug Sept Oct Nov Dec

Quick I.D.: smaller than a robin.
Male: unmistakable, magnificent scarlet body with contrasting black wings and tail; changes in fall to look like female. *Female:* olive-yellow overall; pale brownish flight feathers.
Size: 6¹/₂–7¹/₂ in.

Horned Lark
Eremophila alpestris

Horned Larks are probably most frequently encountered rising up in front of vehicles speeding along country roads. They cut off to the side an instant before a fatal collision, briefly showing off their distinct black outer tail feathers. Horned Larks resort to these near misses because their first instinct when threatened is to outrun their pursuer. Cars can easily overtake these swift runners, however, so these birds take to the air when their first attempt to flee fails.

Late winter is the best time of year to observe these open-country specialists as they congregate in huge flocks on outlying farmland, eating waste grain. Most of these birds are destined to migrate north when the first hints of warmth loosens winter's chilly grip. However, this migration does not mean that our area is free of these birds through summer, because many nest in our open fields and pastures. They are among the earliest of our courting birds, singing their songs and diving dare-devilishly before the snow has all retreated.

Similar Species: Sparrows lack the black facial and throat markings.

Quick I.D.: larger than a sparrow; brown plumage; black bib, mask and 'tiara'; light underparts; white outer edges on black tail feathers; faint yellow throat. *Female:* duller overall; less prominent horns.
Size: 7–8 in.

Jan Feb Mar Apr May Jun Jul Aug Sept Oct Nov Dec

European Starling
Sturnus vulgaris

breeding

In 1922, 32 years after their intentional release in New York's Central Park, European Starlings began to establish themselves in Illinois. Slightly more than a decade later, flocks of over one million birds were being reported. Today, European Starlings are one of the most common birds in Chicago. Their presence is highlighted by astonishing numbers roosting communally during the winter months.

Unfortunately, the expansion of starlings has come at the expense of many of our native birds, including the Purple Martin and the Eastern Bluebird, which are unable to defend nest cavities against the aggressive starlings. While not all birdwatchers are pleased with the presence of this foreigner to our area, starlings have become a permanent fixture in the bird community. If residents are unable to find joy in this bird's mimicry and flocking, they can take some comfort in knowing that starlings now provide a reliable and stable food source for woodland hawks and the Peregrine Falcon.

Similar Species: All blackbirds have long tails and black bills. Purple Martin (p. 85) has a short bill.

Quick I.D.: smaller than a robin; sexes similar; short tail. *Breeding:* dark, glossy plumage; long, yellow bill. *Non-breeding:* dark bill; spotty plumage. *Juvenile:* brown upperparts; gray-brown underparts; brown bill.
Size: 8–9 in.

Jan Feb Mar Apr May Jun Jul Aug Sept Oct Nov Dec

Gray Catbird
Dumetella carolinensis

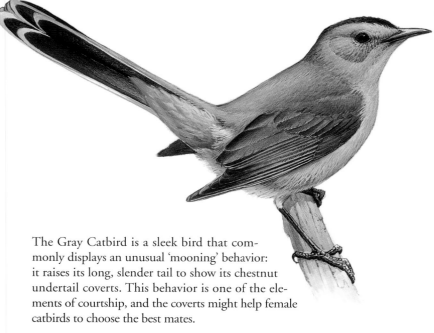

The Gray Catbird is a sleek bird that commonly displays an unusual 'mooning' behavior: it raises its long, slender tail to show its chestnut undertail coverts. This behavior is one of the elements of courtship, and the coverts might help female catbirds to choose the best mates.

The Gray Catbird is a bird of dense shrubs and thickets, and although it's relatively common in appropriate habitats, its distinctive call, rather than the bird itself, is what is most commonly encountered. The Gray Catbird's unmistakable cat-like 'meowing,' for which it's named, can be heard rising from shrubs in forest preserves and shrubby thickets anywhere in our area during May and June.

Similar Species: None.

Quick I.D.: smaller than a robin; sexes similar; slate gray; black cap; chestnut undertail coverts; long, dark tail.
Size: 9 in.

Brown Thrasher
Toxostoma rufum

Male Brown Thrashers have the largest vocal repertoire of any Chicago-area bird—more than 3000 song types. Although thrashers don't have the sweetest voice in Chicago, their loud, continually varying songs are worth listening to. Thrashers will repeat phrases twice, often combining them into complex choruses, such as *dig-it dig-it, hoe-it hoe-it, pull-it-up pull-it-up.*

Brown Thrashers have a reddish-brown back and tail and a heavily streaked breast. They're common in thickets and shrubs, often in close proximity to humans. They're shy birds, however, and they need a lot of coaxing with squeaks and pishes before they pop out into the open. Illinois Beach State Park, during summer, offers ample opportunity to meet this dynamic songster.

Similar Species: Wood Thrush (p. 100) and Veery (p. 99) have shorter tails and straight bills.

Jan Feb Mar Apr May Jun Jul Aug Sept Oct Nov Dec

Quick I.D.: jay-sized; sexes similar; reddish-brown head, back and tail; heavy chest streaking; long, downcurved bill; white wing bars; long tail; no eye ring; yellow eyes.
Size: 11–12 in.

Cedar Waxwing
Bombycilla cedrorum

A faint, high-pitched trill is often your first clue that waxwings are around. Search the treetops to see these cinnamon-crested birds as they dart out in quick bursts, snacking on flying insects. Cedar Waxwings are found in many habitats throughout Chicago, wherever ripe berries provide abundant food supplies.

Cedar Waxwings are most often seen in large flocks in late spring and fall, when they congregate on fruit trees and quickly eat all the berries. Some people remember these visits not only for the birds' beauty, but because fermentation of the fruit occasionally renders the flock flightless from intoxication.

Similar Species: Tufted Titmouse has no yellow on its belly or tail.

Quick I.D.: smaller than a robin; sexes similar; fine, pale brown plumage; small crest; black mask; yellow belly wash; yellow-tipped tail; light under-tail coverts; shiny red (waxy-looking) droplets on wing tips. *Juvenile:* streaky underparts.
Size: 7–8 in.

Jan Feb Mar Apr May Jun Jul Aug Sept Oct Nov Dec

Eastern Towhee
Pipilo erythrophthalmus

This large, cocky sparrow is most often heard before it is seen, scratching away leaves and debris in the dense understory. These are noisy foragers, because Eastern Towhees tend to make the most out of leaf litter scattered beneath second-growth deciduous areas. Deep in the shadows of shrubs, the Eastern Towhee's sharp, *Drink your Teeea* identifies this secretive sparrow.

To best observe this bird, which was formerly grouped with the West's Spotted Towhee (together they were known as the Rufous-sided Towhee), learn a few birding tricks. Squeaking and pishing are irresistible for towhees, which will quickly pop out from the cover to investigate the curious noise.

Similar Species: American Robin (p. 101) is larger and has no white on its chest. Dark-eyed Junco (p. 130) is smaller and has white outer tail feathers.

Jan Feb Mar Apr May Jun Jul Aug Sept Oct Nov Dec

Quick I.D.: smaller than a robin; black head; rufous-colored flanks; black back; white outer tail feathers; white underparts; red eyes.
Male: black head, breast and upperparts.
Female: reddish-brown head, breast and upperparts.
Size: 8–9 in.

American Tree Sparrow
Spizella arborea

The American Tree Sparrow's annual migration into Illinois during late fall is a sign of the changing seasons. For the entire winter, these Arctic nesters decorate the leafless rural shrublands like ornaments on a Christmas tree. As one of the first songbirds to disappear in April and a regular arrival in late October, American Tree Sparrow activities quietly announce the closing of autumn and the opening of spring.

These humble, quiet sparrows often go unnoticed despite their large numbers. American Tree Sparrows occasionally visit city feeders during their migrations and while wintering in the Chicago area, but they never attempt to usurp the surly resident flocks of House Sparrows and House Finches, because these sparrows prefer outlying weedy and fallow fields.

Similar Species: Chipping (p. 123), Field (p. 124) and Swamp (p. 128) sparrows all lack a faint breast spot.

Quick I.D.: large sparrow; sexes similar; red crown; no eyebrow; small, central chest spot, breast otherwise unstreaked; mottled back; grayish bill with yellow lower mandible; white wing bars.
Size: 6 in.

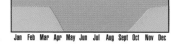

Jan Feb Mar Apr May Jun Jul Aug Sept Oct Nov Dec

Chipping Sparrow
Spizella passerina

Hopping around freshly mowed lawns, the cheery Chipping Sparrow goes about its business unconcerned by the busy world of suburban Chicago. One of the most widespread species in Illinois, the Chipping Sparrow brings birdwatching to those who rarely venture from their homes.

These sparrows nest frequently in our backyards, building their small nest cups with dried vegetation and lining them with animal hair. Chipping Sparrows usually attempt to bring off two broods of young every year in Chicago. Three or four small, greenish-blue eggs are laid in mid-May, and again later near the beginning of July, should conditions prove favorable. These passive birds are delightful neighbors in our backyards, and they demand nothing more than a little privacy around the rose bush, vine tangle or small tree where they have chosen to nest.

Similar Species: American Tree Sparrow (p. 122) is only a winter resident and has a black central chest spot. Swamp Sparrow (p. 128) lacks the clean white, black-lined eyebrow. Field Sparrow (p. 124) has a pink bill and lacks the white eyebrow.

Jan Feb Mar Apr May Jun Jul Aug Sept Oct Nov Dec

Quick I.D.: small sparrow; sexes similar; red crown; white eyebrow; black eye line; clear grayish breast; streaked back.
Size: 5 1/2 in.

Field Sparrow

Spizella pusilla

The innocent, unmarked face of the Field Sparrow gives this common bird a perpetual look of adolescence. Like a teenager prior to his first shave, the Field Sparrow has a soft, wholesome look, highlighted by its pink bill and untainted eyes.

Many sparrows have very descriptive and accurate names, but the Field Sparrow's name is somewhat misleading. An inhabitant of overgrown meadows and bushy areas, Field Sparrows tend to avoid expansive, grassy fields. Their nesting sites are often found away from developments, but not far enough from Brown-headed Cowbirds. These nest parasites can occupy over one-quarter of the nests in our area, affecting the Field Sparrow's reproductive rate. Fortunately, cowbirds have not significantly decreased the population of these tireless singers, who offer their 'ping pong ball' song on hot summer days when most other singers are silenced.

Similar Species: Chipping Sparrow (p. 123) has a white eyebrow and a black eye line. American Tree Sparrow (p. 122) has a dark chest spot and a dark bill.

Quick I.D.: mid-sized sparrow; sexes similar; reddish crown; plain gray underparts; pink bill; light gray eyebrow; rusty brown back; prominent white eye ring.
Size: 5–6 in.

Jan Feb Mar Apr May Jun Jul Aug Sept Oct Nov Dec

Savannah Sparrow
Passerculus sandwichensis

The Savannah Sparrow is a common bird of the open country. Its dull brown plumage and streaked breast conceal it perfectly in the long grasses of native prairie, farms and roadsides. It breeds in fields of weedy annuals and grass along Vollmer Road and in grassy rural areas.

The Savannah Sparrow resorts to flight only as a last alternative: it prefers to run swiftly and inconspicuously through long grass, and it is most often seen darting across roads and open fields. The Savannah Sparrow's distinctive buzzy trill—*tea-tea-tea-teeea today*—and the usual yellow eyebrow and patch in front of each eye are the best ways to distinguish it from the many other grassland sparrows.

Similar Species: Song Sparrow (p. 127) has a breast spot. Vesper Sparrow lacks the yellow lore, has white outer tail feathers and a chestnut shoulder patch, and its song is a buzzy *Here here, there there, Everybody down the hill.*

Jan Feb Mar Apr May Jun Jul Aug Sept Oct Nov Dec

Quick I.D.: small sparrow; sexes similar; streaked underparts and upperparts; mottled brown above; dark cheek; no white outer tail feathers; usually has yellow lores.
Size: 5–6 in.

Fox Sparrow
Passerella iliaca

The Fox Sparrow is a noisy migrant in Chicago's thickets and brambles. Like many other sparrows that spend time in this habitat, the Fox Sparrow is appreciated for its voice more than for its subtle, beautiful plumage. During spring, sit and wait near tangles and brush piles in Chicago's parks, and listen as the Fox Sparrow repeatedly belts out its distinctive musical question: *All I have is what's here dear, will-you-will-you take-it?*

The Fox Sparrow hops under feeders and shrubs noisily scratching at leaf litter like a towhee. It finds these areas to its liking, and this bird is infrequently seen anywhere in our region farther than a quick getaway flight into bushes.

Similar Species: Song Sparrow (p. 127) has a different song and a much lighter color. Hermit Thrush has a slimmer bill and smaller breast spots and lacks the gray in the head.

Quick I.D.: large sparrow; sexes similar; heavy breast streaks; red-brown tail, wings and back; light gray-brown head and nape; very dark overall.
Size: 6¹/₂–7 in.

Jan Feb Mar Apr May Jun Jul Aug Sept Oct Nov Dec

Song Sparrow
Melospiza melodia

The Song Sparrow's drab, heavily streaked plumage doesn't prepare you for its symphonic song, which stands out among Chicago-area songsters in complexity and rhythm. This bird, Chicago's most common native sparrow, seems to sing *hip-hip-hip hooray boys, the spring is here again..*

This year-round resident is encountered in a wide variety of habitats. Song Sparrows are easily found in all seasons among marshes, thickets, brambles, weedy fields and woodland edges. Although these birds are most easily identified by their grayish facial streaks while perched, flying birds will characteristically pump their tails.

Similar Species: Fox Sparrow (p. 126) is very heavily streaked and has a different song. Savannah Sparrow (p. 125) and Lincoln's Sparrow have weaker breast streaks.

Jan Feb Mar Apr May Jun Jul Aug Sept Oct Nov Dec

Quick I.D.: mid-sized sparrow; sexes similar; heavy breast streaks form central spot; brown-red plumage; striped head.

Size: 6–7 in.

Swamp Sparrow
Melospiza georgiana

breeding

Although Swamp Sparrows are fairly common in wetlands in the Chicago area, they are far less visible than their neighboring blackbirds and yellowthroats. Except when the male pounces atop a bulrush or willow branch to sing his sweet, loose trill, the Swamp Sparrow seems perfectly content sealed deep within the world of cattail and grasses.

Swamp Sparrows are the most adaptive of the sparrows in our area to life around water. Like all other sparrows, they are unable to swim, but that is no deterrent to this rufous-crowned skulker. Swamp Sparrows glean much of their insectivorous diet directly from the surface of wetlands, and they construct their sideways nest just a foot above the water line. As if Swamp Sparrows become bored with their concealed lifestyle, they can be readily enticed to quickly pop up to a cattail head in response to a birder's urging squeaks.

Similar Species: Chipping Sparrow (p. 123) has a clean white eyebrow, a black eye line and uniform gray underparts. American Tree Sparrow (p. 122) has a central dark chest spot and a two-toned bill.

Quick I.D.: mid-sized sparrow; sexes similar; gray face; rufous upperparts and wings; streaked back. *Breeding:* red cap; white throat; light gray breast; reddish-brown underparts. *Non-breeding:* streaked, brown cap.
Size: 5¹/₂ in.

Jan Feb Mar Apr May Jun Jul Aug Sept Oct Nov Dec

White-throated Sparrow
Zonotrichia albicollis

The catchy song of the White-throated Sparrow is often on the lips of weekend cottagers returning from the north country. By whistling the distinctive *Oh sweet Canada Canada Canada* to themselves, people bring some of the atmosphere of the northern woods to their Chicago-area homes.

In winter, a few White-throated Sparrows linger in the city, where birdfeeders provide them with a steady supply of seed without much physical exertion. This bird's striped head and white throat, as well as its wild song ringing in the steep-walled skyscraper canyons during our winter, allow this forest breeder to stand out.

Similar Species: White-crowned Sparrow lacks the white throat and has a pink bill.

Jan Feb Mar Apr May Jun Jul Aug Sept Oct Nov Dec

Quick I.D.: large sparrow; sexes similar; black and white–striped head; white throat; unstreaked, light gray breast; yellow lore; rusty-brown upperparts; tan phase has brownish, rather than white, streaks on head.
Size: 6¹/₂–7 in.

Dark-eyed Junco

Junco hyemalis

Dark-eyed Juncos occur as abundant migrants and winter visitors throughout the Chicago area. The Dark-eyed Junco is a ground dweller, and it is frequently seen as it flushes from the undergrowth along wooded trails in Chicago's parks and under suburban shrubbery. The distinctive white outer tail feathers will flash in alarm as the bird flies down a narrow path before disappearing into a thicket.

In spring, Dark-eyed Juncos sing their descending trills, which are often easily mistaken with those of the Chipping Sparrow. The confusion can build, because both the junco and the sparrow occur in similar habitats, so a confirmation of identity usually requires a visual search. The junco's distinctive smacking call and its habit of double-scratching at forest litter also help identify it. Juncos are frequent guests at birdfeeders throughout Chicago, usually cleaning up the forgotten seed that has fallen to the ground.

Similar Species: Eastern Towhee (p. 121) is larger and has conspicuous rufous sides. Brown-headed Cowbird (p. 135) lacks the white outer tail feathers and white belly.

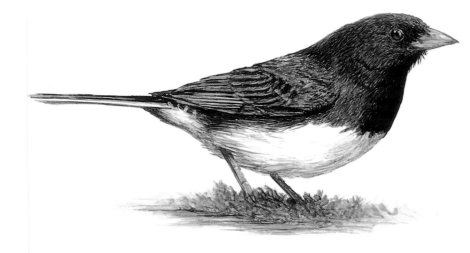

Quick I.D.: large sparrow; slate gray; light-colored bill; white outer tail feathers; white belly. *Female:* somewhat duller.
Size: 5–6¹/₂ in.

Bobolink

Dolichonyx oryzivorus

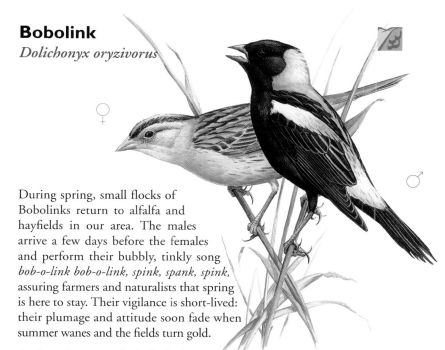

During spring, small flocks of Bobolinks return to alfalfa and hayfields in our area. The males arrive a few days before the females and perform their bubbly, tinkly song *bob-o-link bob-o-link, spink, spank, spink,* assuring farmers and naturalists that spring is here to stay. Their vigilance is short-lived: their plumage and attitude soon fade when summer wanes and the fields turn gold.

At first glimpse, Bobolinks look every bit a sparrow, especially the drab females, which lack the male's style—he looks as though he's wearing a tuxedo backwards. But these are not sparrows at all; rather, they are blackbirds— evident by their polygynous breeding strategy. Males that acquire prime hayfields can mate with and defend several nesting females.

The fall migration of Bobolinks is one of the most spectacular and longest of all songbirds. Birds leaving Illinois flock with others farther south and soon number in the thousands. These flocks once descended on rice crops in the southeast states, where they were known as 'rice birds.' Bobolinks were so effectively controlled by rice farmers and the elimination of hayfields and prairie remnants that the populations that occur in the Chicago area continue to recover to this day.

Similar Species: Brown-headed Cowbird (p. 135) has a black back. Sparrows tend to lack the pointy tail feathers.

Jan Feb Mar Apr May Jun Jul Aug Sept Oct Nov Dec

Quick I.D.: larger than a sparrow; pointed tail feathers. *Breeding male:* black head and body; buffy nape; white rump. *Female* and *Non-breeding male:* buffy brown body; dark crown streaks; dark eye line.
Size: 6–8 in.

Red-winged Blackbird
Agelaius phoeniceus

From March through July, no marsh is free from the loud calls and bossy, aggressive nature of the Red-winged Blackbird. A springtime walk around any Chicago-area marshland will be accompanied by this bird's loud, raspy and persistent *konk-a-reee* or *eat my CHEEEzies* song. During fall migration, the shorelines of Lake Michigan can become congested with thousands of these birds as they flock their way southwards.

The male's bright red shoulders (or 'epaulets') are his most important tool in the strategic and intricate displays he uses to defend his territory from rivals and to attract a mate. In experiments, males whose red shoulders were painted black soon lost their territories to rivals they had previously defeated. The female's interest lies not in the individual combatants, but in nesting habitat, and a male that can successfully defend a large area of dense cattails will breed with many females. After the females have built their concealed nests and laid their eggs, the male continues his persistent vigil.

Similar Species: Brewer's Blackbird and Brown-headed Cowbird (p. 135) lack the red shoulder patches.

Quick I.D.: smaller than a robin. *Male:* all-black plumage; large, red patch bordered by creamy yellow on each shoulder. *Female:* brown overall; heavily streaked; hint of red on shoulder.
Size: 7¹/₂–9¹/₂ in.

Jan Feb Mar Apr May Jun Jul Aug Sept Oct Nov Dec

Eastern Meadowlark

Sturnella magna

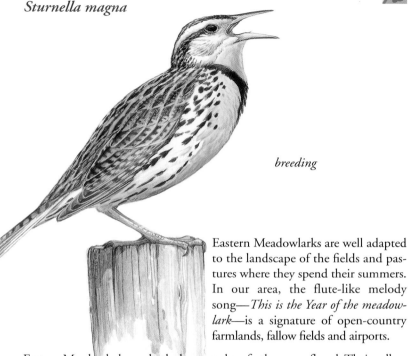

breeding

Eastern Meadowlarks are well adapted to the landscape of the fields and pastures where they spend their summers. In our area, the flute-like melody song—*This is the Year of the meadowlark*—is a signature of open-country farmlands, fallow fields and airports.

Eastern Meadowlarks are both showy and perfectly camouflaged. Their yellow sweater with the black V-neck and their white outer tail feathers serve to attract mates—and predators. Potential meadowlark mates face one another, raise their bills high and perform a grassland ballet. Oddly, the colorful breast and white tail feathers are also used to attract the attention of potential predators. Foxes, hawks or falcons focus on these bold features in pursuit, so their prey mysteriously disappears into the grass whenever the meadowlark chooses to turn its back or fold away its white tail flags.

Similar Species: Savannah Sparrow (p. 125) is much smaller and lacks the yellow chest and white outer tail feathers. Dickcissel (p. 142) is smaller and lacks the white outer tail feathers. Western Meadowlark lacks the dark reddish-brown upperparts.

Quick I.D.: robin-sized; sexes similar; mottled brown upperparts; black 'V' on chest; yellow throat and belly; white outer tail feathers; striped head.
Size: 8–10 in.

Jan Feb Mar Apr May Jun Jul Aug Sept Oct Nov Dec

Common Grackle

Quiscalus quiscula

The Common Grackle is a noisy and cocky bird that prefers to feed on the ground in open areas. Birdfeeders in rural areas can attract large numbers of these blackish birds, whose cranky disposition drives away most other birds (even the quarrelsome Blue Jay and House Sparrow). The Common Grackle is easily identified by its long tail, large bill and dark plumage, which can shine with hues of green, purple and blue in bright light.

The Common Grackle is a poor but spirited singer. Usually while perched in a shrub, a male grackle will slowly take a deep breath that inflates his chest and causes his feathers to rise. Then he closes his eyes and gives out a loud, surprising *swaaaack*. Despite our perception of the Common Grackle's musical weakness, following his 'song' the male smugly and proudly poses with his bill held high, to display his dominance.

Similar Species: Brown-headed Cowbird (p. 135), American Crow (p. 90) and Rusty Blackbird have relatively shorter tails.

Quick I.D.: jay-sized; sexes similar; glossy black plumage with purple and brown iridescence; long, keeled tail; large bill.
Size: 11–13 in.

Jan Feb Mar Apr May Jun Jul Aug Sept Oct Nov Dec

Brown-headed Cowbird
Molothrus ater

Brown-headed Cowbirds have been well established within the matrix of the region's bird life since they followed the historic wanderings of bison. This gregarious bird is very common in outlying agricultural areas, and it can be seen in large numbers during migration along Lake Michigan.

The Brown-headed Cowbird is infamous for being a nest parasite—female cowbirds do not incubate their own eggs, but instead lay them in the nests of many songbirds. Cowbird eggs have a short incubation period, and the cowbird chicks often hatch before the host songbird's own chicks. Many songbirds do not recognize that the fast-growing cowbird chick is not one of their own, and they will continue to feed it even after the cowbird chick has grown larger than the songbird. In its efforts to get as much food as possible, a cowbird chick might squeeze the host's own young out of the nest. The populations of many songbird species in Illinois have been devastated in part by the activities of the Brown-headed.

Similar Species: Common Grackle (p. 134) has a relatively longer tail. Rusty Blackbird has a slimmer body and yellow eyes.

Jan Feb Mar Apr May Jun Jul Aug Sept Oct Nov Dec

Quick I.D.: smaller than a robin. *Male:* metallic-looking, glossy black plumage; soft brown head; dark eyes. *Female:* brownish gray overall; dark eyes; slight chest streaks.
Size: 6–8 in.

Baltimore Oriole

Icterus galbula

Although it is a common summer resident of city parks and cottonwood and willow valleys, the Baltimore Oriole is seldom seen. Unlike the American Robin, which inhabits the human domain of shrubs and lawns, the Baltimore Oriole nests and feeds in the tallest deciduous trees available. The vacant nest, which is easily seen on bare trees in fall, is often the only indication that a pair of orioles summered in an area. This bird's hanging, six-inch-deep, pouch-like nest is deceptively strong.

The male Baltimore Oriole's striking, Halloween-like, black-and-orange plumage flashes like embers amidst the dense foliage of the treetops, while its slow purposeful *Peter Peter here here Peter Peter* song drips to the forest floor.

From mid-May to mid-July, mature deciduous forests or second-growth parkland throughout our area should produce at least one of these beautiful birds for oriole-starved Chicago-area birdwatchers.

Similar Species: Orchard Oriole is smaller and has chestnut rather than orange plumage.

Quick I.D.: smaller than a robin. *Male:* brilliant orange belly, flanks, outer tail feathers and rump; black hood, wings and tail. *Female:* yellow-green upperparts; yellow throat; faint hood.
Size: 7–8 in.

Jan Feb Mar Apr May Jun Jul Aug Sept Oct Nov Dec

House Finch
Carpodacus mexicanus

The House Finch is one of the earliest voices to announce the coming of spring. These common city and country birds sing their warbling melodies from backyards, parks and suburban TV antennas.

During the 1920s and 1930s, these birds, native to the American Southwest, were popular cage birds, and they were sold across the continent as 'Hollywood Finches.' Illegal releases of the caged birds and expansion from their historic range have resulted in two separate distributions in North America, which have recently converged. House Finches found in Illinois spread from the east and arrived in 1972. They are now well established here, nesting in house gutters and flower baskets.

Similar Species: Male Purple Finch is raspberry-colored and has unstreaked undertail coverts, and the female has a brown cheek contrasting with a white eyebrow and a mustache stripe.

Jan Feb Mar Apr May Jun Jul Aug Sept Oct Nov Dec

Quick I.D.: sparrow-sized; squared tail.
Male: deep red forehead, eyebrow and throat; buffy gray belly; brown cheek; streaked sides and undertail coverts. *Female:* brown overall; streaked underparts; no eyebrow.
Size: 5–6 in.

American Goldfinch
Carduelis tristis

breeding

♀

♂

In spring, the American Goldfinch swings over fields in its distinctive, undulating flight, and it fills the air with its jubilant *po-ta-to chip* call. This bright, cheery songbird is commonly seen during summer in weedy fields, roadsides and backyards, where it feeds on thistle seeds. The American Goldfinch delays nesting until June or July to ensure a dependable source of insects, thistles and dandelion seeds to feed its young.

The American Goldfinch is a common backyard bird in parts of the Chicago area, and it can be attracted to feeding stations that offer a supply of niger seed. Goldfinches are easily bullied at feeders by larger sparrows and finches, but only goldfinches and Pine Siskins invert for food, so a special finch feeder with openings below the perches is ideal for ensuring a steady stream of what some people call 'wild canaries.'

Similar Species: Yellow Warbler (p. 106) does not have black on its forehead or wings. Evening Grosbeak is much larger and has broad white wing patches.

Quick I.D.: smaller than a sparrow. *Breeding male:* black forehead, wings and tail; canary yellow body; wings show white in flight. *Female* and *Non-breeding male:* no black on forehead; yellow-green overall; black wings and tail.
Size: 4¹/₂–5¹/₂ in.

Jan Feb Mar Apr May Jun Jul Aug Sept Oct Nov Dec

Northern Cardinal
Cardinalis cardinalis

♀

♂

The gallantry of the Northern Cardinal is not only found in its renowned attire—this species's pair bond is one of the most faithful of Chicago's resident birds. Never far from one another, male and female cardinals softly vocalize to one another not only through the breeding season, but year-round, as if sharing sweet nothings. The ritualized beak-to-beak feeding re-inforces the romantic appeal of these easily identifiable birds. Although the regal male does little more than warble to the female while she constructs the nest, his parental duties will soon keep him busy. After the eggs have hatched, the nestlings and the brooding female will remain in the nest while the male provides much of the food for the family.

The state bird of Illinois is common at backyard feeders. As if grateful to residents with backyard feeders, Northern Cardinals offer up their bubbly *What cheer! What cheer! Birdie-birdie-birdie What cheer!* and enliven neighborhoods.

Similar Species: Scarlet Tanager (p. 115) has black wings and tail.

Jan Feb Mar Apr May Jun Jul Aug Sept Oct Nov Dec

Quick I.D.: smaller than a robin. *Male:* unmistakable; red overall; black mask and throat; pointed crest; red, conical bill. *Female:* similar to male, except plumage quite a bit duller.
Size: 8–9 in.

Rose-breasted Grosbeak
Pheucticus ludovicianus

Male Rose-breasted Grosbeaks have a voice that matches their magnificent plumage. Showing not the least concern for would-be predators, male Rose-breasted Grosbeaks flaunt their song and plumage in treetop performances. This common songster's boldness does not go unnoticed by the appreciative birding community, which eagerly anticipates the male's annual spring concert. The male's outlandish plumage compensates for that of his unassuming mate, which lacks the formal dress but shares her partner's musical talents. Whether the nest is incubated by the male or female, the developing young are continually introduced into the world of song by the brooding parent.

This neotropical migrant nests in mature deciduous forest and second-growth shrubby areas, such as those found in parts of Ryerson Conservation Area or in less developed urban areas.

Similar Species: Male is distinctive. Female is similar to female Purple Finch and sparrows, but is generally larger.

Quick I.D.: smaller than a robin. *Male:* black hood; rose breast; black back and wings; white rump; white wing bars; light-colored, conical bill. *Female:* heavily streaked with brown; white eyebrow; pinkish or whitish, conical bill; light throat.
Size: 7–8 in.

Jan Feb Mar Apr May Jun Jul Aug Sept Oct Nov Dec

Indigo Bunting
Passerina cyanea

Metallic-blue male Indigo Buntings are frequently encountered singing all day long along open areas of overgrown fields and forest edges. Perched atop a shrub or thicket, the males conduct elaborate tactical maneuvers with song. With rival males only a voice away, Indigo Buntings call continuously through the day to maintain superiority over their peers. Neighboring males copy and learn from one another, producing 'song territories.' Each male within a song territory has personal variation to *fire-fire, where-where, here-here, see-it see-it,* producing his own acoustic fingerprint.

Indigo Buntings are widespread throughout our area during summer, popping out of dense bushes anywhere along roadsides and park edges. They build a small nest cup low to the ground, in an upright crotch amid a shrubby tangle. Once nesting duties are complete, these buntings are commonly seen along railroad tracks, beginning their exodus in August, following a partial molt.

Similar Species: Eastern Bluebird (p. 98) is larger, has a red breast and slimmer body, and lacks the wing bars. Female is similar to many female sparrows, but lacks the streaking.

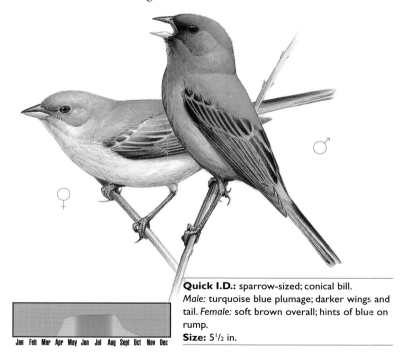

Quick I.D.: sparrow-sized; conical bill. *Male:* turquoise blue plumage; darker wings and tail. *Female:* soft brown overall; hints of blue on rump.
Size: 5¹/₂ in.

Jan Feb Mar Apr May Jun Jul Aug Sept Oct Nov Dec

Dickcissel

Spiza americana

breeding

In an affectionate comparison of habitat, dress and behavior, the bright Dickcissel is often referred to as a mini-meadowlark. Like its much larger prairie ally, the Dickcissel can be seen singing atop posts and perches along the open country of Vollmer Road. Turning your ear in spring to the surrounding fields, you will be treated to the tell-tale song of the bird, an onomatopoeic *dick dick ciss, ciss ciss ...*

This distinctive song is easily heard throughout late spring, because this grassland-lover sings into the heat of the day, long after its chorus mates have been silenced. When Dickcissels' intentions veer away from reproduction and their singing stops, the fields once dominated by these large sparrows seem perfectly empty. At this time of year it is only when Dickcissels pass overhead that they are easily noticed, because they continually produce an electric buzzer–like *bzrrrt!*

Similar Species: Eastern Meadowlark (p. 133) is larger overall and has white outer tail feathers.

Quick I.D.: large sparrow; yellow eyebrow and breast; gray cheek; heavy bill; mottled brown back; chestnut shoulder; dark legs. *Male:* black bib. *Female:* duller overall; no black bib.
Size: 6–7 in.

Jan Feb Mar Apr May Jun Jul Aug Sept Oct Nov Dec

House Sparrow
Passer domesticus

This common backyard bird often confuses novice birdwatchers because females and immatures can be very nondescript. The male is relatively conspicuous—he has a black bib, a gray cap and white lines trailing down from his mouth (as though he has spilled milk on himself)—and he sings a continuous series of *cheep-cheep-cheeps*. The best field mark for the female, apart from her pale eyebrows, is that there are no distinctive field marks.

The House Sparrow was introduced to North America in the 1850s to control insects. Although this familiar bird can consume great quantities of insects, the majority of its diet is seeds, and it has become somewhat of a pest. The House Sparrow's aggressive nature usurps several native songbird species from nesting cavities, and its boldness often drives other birds away from backyard feeders. The House Sparrow and the European Starling are now two of the most common birds in cities and on farms, and they are a constant reminder of the negative impact of human introductions on natural systems.

Similar Species: Male is distinctive. Female is similar to female sparrows and finches, but tends to lack any distinctive markings.

Jan Feb Mar Apr May Jun Jul Aug Sept Oct Nov Dec

Quick I.D.: mid-sized sparrow; brownish-gray belly. *Male:* black throat; gray forehead; white jowl; chestnut nape. *Female:* plain; pale eyebrow; mottled wings.
Size: 5^1/$_2$–6^1/$_2$ in.

Watching Birds

Identifying your first new bird can be so satisfying that you just might become addicted to birdwatching. Luckily, birdwatching does not have to be expensive; it all hinges on how involved in this hobby you want to get. Setting up a simple backyard feeder is an easy way to get to know the birds sharing your neighborhood, and some people simply find birdwatching a pleasant way to complement a nightly walk with the dog or a morning commute into work.

Many people enjoy going to urban parks and feeding the wild birds that have become accustomed to humans. This activity provides people with intimate contact with urban-dwelling birds, but remember that birdseed, or better yet the birds' natural food items, are much healthier for the birds than bread and crackers.

SEASONS OF BIRDWATCHING

Spring

Spring is often the most favored season for birders, many of whom will be enthusiastically searching for early migrants at the first sign of warm weather. Each spring, Chicago is treated to a spectacular migration display as nearby rivers, valleys and shorelines funnel birds along their migration routes. By early March, large congregations of waterfowl are settling on open bodies of water, including Lake Michigan. As waterfowl numbers begin to decline, egrets and herons slowly move into the area, and by late April and early May, many of them have already settled into the cattails of local lakes and marshes, such as McGinnis Slough and McKee Marsh. Throughout late April and May, shorebirds pass through the area, followed closely by the long-anticipated landbird migration. For three weeks in May, local tracts of deciduous woodland are teeming with the bright and colorful movements of flycatchers, thrushes, vireos, warblers and sparrows. By the end of the month, however, many birds have departed for their northern breeding grounds or have already settled in their respective territories.

Summer

The Chicago area boasts an impressive list of breeding birds, and although the pace of avian life slows down during the summer months, there is still considerable activity. Many woodpeckers, including the Red-headed, Red-bellied,

Downy and Hairy, nest in and around the Chicago area, excavating cavities in old or decaying deciduous trees. Various parks host breeding raptors, such as the American Kestrel and the Eastern Screech-Owl, which choose to nest in woodland cavities, especially abandoned woodpecker holes. The lush canopies of woodland parks are popular nesting locations for many warblers and other songbirds. Some birds, such as the Warbling Vireo and the Scarlet Tanager, nest high in the treetops, but others, such as the Ovenbird, always build their nests among the leafy undergrowth of the forest bottom. Chicago's waterfront is also a great place to view waterbirds during the warmer months.

Fall

The fall migrations, beginning as early as July and extending into December, are less concentrated than in spring, but they last much longer. Shorebirds are the first to travel south through our area, followed closely by flights of landbirds, most in their dull fall plumage. Landbird migration begins in late August and lasts into October and November. Fall is the time to watch great numbers of hawks passing overhead on their way south. A favorite hawk-watching locale is along the western shore of Lake Michigan at Illinois Beach State Park. In October, waterfowl concentrations are at their peak, and numbers in the thousands are not unheard-of. During fall, many of the ducks, shorebirds, gulls and warblers have acquired frustratingly similar plumages, but this season has its own benefits: the prolonged migratory season provides a much longer time for observing all sorts of interesting birds.

Winter

The winter months are a good time to find a variety of waterbirds along Chicago's lakefront. Many areas that do not freeze over attract Canada Geese, American Black Ducks, Oldsquaws, Common Mergansers and a variety of gulls, among others. A visit to any woodland park will most often reward the birder with views of many common wintering and year-round species, such as the Black-capped Chickadee, the Northern Cardinal, the American Goldfinch and, during the most mild winters, the Song Sparrow. Woodlands are also home to resident species of woodpeckers and owls, many of which inhabit cavities in old trees and snags. Red-bellied and Downy woodpeckers are found year-round in forested areas of the Chicago region, and owls, such as the Great Horned Owl and Eastern Screech-Owl, are often more conspicuous during the winter months. Winter is also the time for birdfeeders, and a good day might attract a wide diversity of species to backyards or neighborhoods.

BIRDING OPTICS

Most people who are interested in birdwatching will eventually buy a pair of binoculars. They help you identify key bird characteristics, such as plumage and bill color, and they also help you identify other birders! Birdwatchers are a friendly sort, and a chat among birders is all part of the experience.

You'll use your binoculars often, so select a pair that will contribute to the quality of your birdwatching experience—they don't have to be expensive. If you need help deciding which pair is right for you, talk to other birdwatchers or to someone at your local nature center.

One of the first things you'll notice about binoculars (apart from the price extremes) is that they all have two numbers associated with them (8x40, for example). The first number, which is always the smallest, is the magnification (how large the bird will appear), while the second is the size (in millimeters) of the objective lens (the larger end). It might seem important at first to get the highest magnification possible, but a reasonable magnification of 7x to 8x is optimal for all-purpose birding: it draws you fairly close to most birds without causing too much shaking. Some shaking happens to everyone; to overcome it, rest the binoculars against a support, such as a partner's shoulder or a tree.

The size of the objective lens is really a question of birding conditions and weight. Because wider lenses (40–50 mm) will bring in more light, these are preferred for birding in low-light situations (like before sunrise or after sunset). If these aren't the conditions that you will be pursuing, a light pair that has an objective lens diameter of less than 30 mm might be the right choice. Because binoculars tend to become heavy after hanging around your neck all day, the compact models are becoming increasingly popular. If you have a pair that is heavy, you can purchase a strap that redistributes part of the weight to the shoulders and lower back.

Another valuable piece of equipment is a spotting scope. It is very useful when you are trying to sight waterfowl, shorebirds or soaring raptors, but it is really of no use if you are intent on seeing forest birds. A good spotting scope has a magnification of around 40x. It has a sturdy tripod or a window mount for the car. Be wary of non-birding telescopes, because they are designed for seeing stars, and their magnification is too great for birdwatching. One of the advantages of having a scope is that you will be able to see far-off birds. By setting up in one spot (or by not even leaving your car) you can observe faraway flocks that would be little more than specks in your binoculars.

With these simple pieces of equipment (none of which is truly essential) and this handy field guide, anyone can enjoy birds in their area. After experiencing the thrill of a couple of hard-won identifications, you will find yourself taking your binoculars on walks, drives and trips to the beach, forest and field. As rewards accumulate with experience, you may find the books and photos piling up and your trips being planned just to see birds!

BIRDING BY EAR

Sometimes, bird *listening* can be more effective than bird *watching*. The technique of birding by ear is gaining popularity, because listening for birds can be more efficient, productive and rewarding than waiting for a visual confirmation. Birds have distinctive songs that they use to resolve territorial disputes, and sound is therefore a useful way to identify species. It is particularly useful when trying to watch some of the smaller forest-dwelling birds. Their size and often indistinct plumage can make a visual search of the forest canopy frustrating. To facilitate auditory searches, catchy paraphrases are included in the descriptions of many of the birds. If the paraphrase just doesn't seem to work for you (they are often a personal thing) be creative and try to find one that fits. By spending time playing the song over in your head, fitting words to it, the voices of birds soon become as familiar as the voices of family members. Many excellent CDs and tapes are available at bookstores and wild-bird stores for the songs of the birds in your area.

BIRDFEEDERS

They're messy, they can be costly, and they're sprouting up in neighborhoods everywhere. Feeding birds has become a common pastime in residential communities all over North America. Although the concept is fairly straightforward, as with anything else involving birds, feeders can become quite elaborate.

The great advantage to feeding birds is that neighborhood chickadees, jays, juncos and finches are enticed into regular visits. Don't expect birds to arrive at your feeder as soon as you set it up; it can take weeks for a few regulars to incorporate your yard into their daily routine. As the popularity of your feeder grows, the number of visiting birds will increase and more species will arrive. You will notice that your feeder is busier during winter, when natural foods are less abundant. You can increase the odds of a good avian turnout by using a variety of feeders and seeds. When a number of birds habitually visit your yard, maintaining the feeder becomes a responsibility, because the birds might rely on it as a regular food source.

Larger birds tend to enjoy feeding on platforms or on the ground; smaller birds are comfortable on hanging seed dispensers. Certain seeds tend to attract specific birds; nature centers and wild-bird supply stores are the best places to ask how to attract a favorite species. It's mainly seed eaters that are attracted to backyards; some birds have no interest in feeders. Only the most committed birdwatcher will try to attract birds that are insect eaters, berry eaters or, in some extreme cases, scavengers!

The location of the feeder can influence the amount of business it receives from the neighborhood birds. Because birds are wild, they are instinctively wary, and they are unlikely to visit an area where they might come under attack. When putting up your feeder, think like a bird. A good, clear view with convenient escape routes is always appreciated. Cats like birdfeeders that are close to the ground and within pouncing distance from a bush; obviously, birds don't. Above all, a birdfeeder should be in view of a favorite window, where you can sit and enjoy the rewarding interaction of your appreciative feathered guests.

CHICAGO-AREA BIRD SOCIETIES

There are many bird societies and clubs you can join in the Chicago area. We have listed some of the larger ones here:

Chicago Audubon Society
5801-C North Pulaski Road
Chicago, IL 60646-6057
phone: (773) 539-6793
e-mail: chicago_audubon@juno.com

Illinois Audubon Society
425 B North Gilbert
Danville, IL 61834
phone: (217) 446-5085

Chicago Ornithological Society
c/o Geoff Williamson, President
4016 N. Clarendon Ave., #3N
Chicago, IL 60613
phone: (773) 935-8439

Illinois Ornithological Society
P.O. Box 1971
Evanston, IL 60204-1971
website: http://www.chias.org/ios/

Evanston North Shore Bird Club
P.O. Box 1313
Evanston, IL 60204

Du Page Birding Club
c/o Nagendra Kolluru
4308 Nutmeg Lane, #244
Lisle, IL 60532

If you want up-to-date information on birds in the Chicago area, there are two local rare bird alerts:

Chicago Area Rare Bird Alert: (847) 265-2118

Du Page County Rare Bird Alert: (630) 406-8111

Glossary

accipiter: a forest hawk (genus *Accipiter*); characterized by a long tail and short, rounded wings; feeds mostly on birds.

brood: *n.* a family of young from one hatching; *v.* sit on eggs so as to hatch them.

corvid: a member of the crow family (Corvidae); includes crows, jays, magpies and ravens.

covey: a brood or flock of partridges, quails or grouse.

crop: an enlargement of the esophagus; serves as a storage structure and (in pigeons) has glands that produce secretions.

dabbling: a foraging technique used by ducks, where the head and neck are submerged but the body and tail remain on the water's surface; dabbling ducks can usually walk easily on land, can take off without running and have brightly colored speculums.

dimorphism: the existence of two distinct forms of a species, such as between the sexes.

eclipse: the dull, female-like plumage that male ducks briefly acquire after molting from their breeding plumage.

elbow patch: a dark spot at the bend of the outstretched wing, seen from below.

flycatching: a feeding behavior where the bird leaves a perch, snatches an insect in mid-air and returns to the same perch; also known as 'hawking' or 'sallying.'

fledgling: a young chick that has just acquired its permanent flight feathers but is still dependent on its parents.

flushing: a behavior where frightened birds explode into flight in response to a disturbance.

gape: the size of the mouth opening.

irruption: a sporadic mass migration of birds into a non-breeding area.

leading edge: the front edge of the wing.

lore: the small patch between the eye and the bill.

molting: the periodic replacement of worn out feathers (often twice a year).

morphology: the science of form and shape.

nape: the back of the neck.

neotropical migrant: a bird that nests in North America but overwinters in the New World tropics.

niche: an ecological role filled by a species.

open country: a landscape that is primarily not forested.

parasitism: a relationship between two species where one benefits at the expense of the other.

phylogenetics: a method of classifying animals that puts the oldest ancestral groups before those that have arisen more recently.

pishing: making a sound to attract birds by saying *pishhh* as loudly and as wetly as possible.

polyandrous: having a mating strategy where one female breeds with several males.

polygynous: having a mating strategy where one male breeds with several females.

plucking post: a perch habitually used by an accipiter for plucking feathers from its prey.

raptor: a carnivorous (meat-eating) bird; includes eagles, hawks, falcons and owls.

rufous: rusty red in color.

speculum: a brightly colored patch in the wings of many dabbling ducks.

squeaking: making a sound to attract birds by loudly kissing the back of the hand, or by using a specially design squeaky bird call.

talons: the claws of birds of prey.

understory: the shrub or thicket layer beneath a canopy of trees.

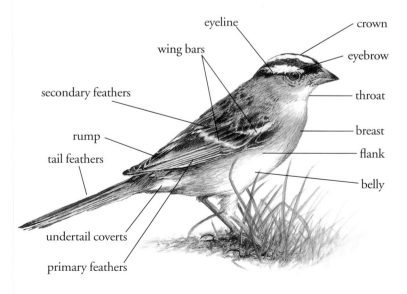

References

American Ornithologists' Union. 1983–97. *Check-list of North American Birds.* 6th ed. (and its supplements). American Ornithologists' Union, Washington, D.C.

Bohlen, H. D. 1989. *The Birds of Illinois.* Indiana University Press, Bloomington.

Chicago Audubon Society. 1998. *Birds of The Greater Chicago Area.* 2nd ed. Chicago Audubon Society, Chicago.

Ehrlich, P. R., D. S. Dobkin and D. Wheye. 1988. *The Birder's Handbook.* Fireside, New York.

Evans, H. E. 1993. *Pioneer Naturalists: The Discovery and Naming of North American Plants and Animals.* Henry Holt and Company, New York.

Farrand, J., ed. 1983. *The Audubon Society Master Guide to Birding.* 3 vols. Alfred A. Knopf, New York.

Gotch, A. F. 1981. *Birds: Their Latin Names Explained.* Blandford Press, Dorset, England.

Mearns, B., and R. Mearns. 1992. *Audubon to Xantus: The Lives of Those Commemorated in North American Bird Names.* Academic Press, San Diego.

Mlodinow, S. 1984. *Chicago Area Birds.* Chicago Review Press, Chicago.

National Audubon Society. 1971–95. *American Birds.* Vols. 25–48.

Reader's Digest Association. *Book of North American Birds.* The Reader's Digest Association, Pleasantville, New York.

Robbins, C. S., B. Brunn and H. S. Zim. 1966. *Birds of North America.* Golden Press, New York.

Scott, S. S. 1987. *Field Guide to the Birds of North America.* National Geographic Society, Washington, D.C.

Terres, J. K. 1995. *The Audubon Society Encyclopedia of North American Birds.* Wings Books, New York.

Checklist of Chicago-area Birds

The following checklist is reprinted from *Birds of the Greater Chicago Area: A Season Checklist* (1982, rev. 1998), which was compiled for the Chicago Audubon Society by Alan Richardson, Richard Biss, William DeBaets, Homer Eshbaugh, David B. Johnson, Jeffrey Sanders and Alan Stokie.

This checklist includes 313 species of birds that have been reported in the greater Chicago area since 1970. The species are listed in taxonomic order (in accordance with the 41st supplement [July 1997] of the American Ornithologists' Association's *Check-list of North American Birds*). A blank line separates each family of birds. This checklist does not include species that have been reported fewer than 10 times since 1970 and are not normally expected to be present.

For the purpose of this checklist, the 'greater Chicago area' includes

Illinois: Cook, DuPage, Grundy, Kane, Lake, McHenry and Will counties

Indiana: Lake, LaPorte and Porter counties; Willow Slough Fish and Wildlife Area (Newton County); and Jasper-Pulaski State Fish and Wildlife Area (Jasper and Pulaski counties)

Wisconsin: Kenosha and Racine counties.

The checklist has been divided into six seasons to denote the differences between early and late migration periods. Note that our dates are approximate and weather dependent.

ES = Early Spring (11 March to 20 April)
LS = Late Spring (21 April to 10 June)
Su = Summer (11 June to 20 August)
EF = Early Fall (21 August to 30 September)
LF = Late Fall (1 October to 30 November)
Wi = Winter (1 December to 10 March)

Seasonal abundance:

A = Abundant (certain to be found in good numbers in several habitats)
C = Common (certain to be found in good numbers in suitable habitat)
F = Fairly Common (likely to be found in small numbers in suitable habitat)
U = Uncommon (possible to be found in small numbers in suitable habitat)
R = Rare (unlikely to be found, even in suitable habitat)
O = Occasional (one to five birds found in most years)
a = Accidental (one to five birds found in some years)

Other checklist notations:

* = Nesting (known to nest *regularly* in the area)
° = Nesting (has nested in the area, but not regularly)
l = Local (occurs only, or more commonly, in certain areas)
v = Variable (varies in presence and numbers from year to year)

	ES	LS	Su	EF	LF	Wi
Red-throated Loon	O	a	a	-	O	a
Common Loon	F	R	a	O	F	O
Pied-billed Grebe *	F	C	F	C	F	O
Horned Grebe	F	U	a	R	F	O
Red-necked Grebe	O	-	-	a	O	O
Eared Grebe °	O	O	a	O	O	a
Western Grebe	a	-	-	-	O	a
American White Pelican	O	O	O	O	O	a
Double-crested Cormorant *	F	C	C	C	C	O
American Bittern °	O	R	O	R	a	-
Least Bittern *	a	R	U	R	a	-
Great Blue Heron *	F	C	C	C	F	R
Great Egret *	U	C	C	C	U	-
Snowy Egret	-	O	O	O	a	-
Little Blue Heron	a	O	O	O	a	-
Tricolored Heron	-	a	a	a	-	-
Cattle Egret ° (l)	a	R	R	O	a	-
Green Heron *	O	F	F	U	R	a
Black-crowned Night-Heron *	U	C	C	C	R	O
Yellow-crowned Night-Heron *	a	R	R	R	a	-
Turkey Vulture *	U	U	U	U	R	a
Greater White-fronted Goose	R	a	-	a	R	O
Snow Goose	U	a	a	a	U	O
Ross's Goose	a	-	-	-	a	a
Canada Goose *	A	A	A	A	A	A
Brant	a	a	-	-	a	a
Mute Swan *	U	U	U	U	U	U
Tundra Swan	U	a	-	-	U	O
Wood Duck *	F	F	F	F	F	R
Gadwall	F	R	R	R	C	R
Eurasian Wigeon	a	a	-	-	a	a
American Wigeon	C	U	a	U	C	R
American Black Duck °	F	R	O	R	F	F
Mallard *	C	C	C	C	C	C
Blue-winged Teal *	F	F	F	C	F	a
Northern Shoveler °	F	F	R	U	F	O
Northern Pintail °	R	O	O	R	U	R
Green-winged Teal	U	R	R	R	F	R
Canvasback	U	a	a	-	U	O
Redhead °	F	R	O	R	F	R
Ring-necked Duck	C	U	a	a	C	U
Greater Scaup	C	R	a	a	C	F
Lesser Scaup	C	U	a	a	C	U
King Eider	-	-	-	a	a	a
Harlequin Duck	O	a	-	-	O	O
Surf Scoter	O	O	-	a	U	O
White-winged Scoter	R	a	-	a	U	U

	ES	LS	Su	EF	LF	Wi
Black Scoter	O	a	-	a	U	O
Oldsquaw	U	a	-	-	F	F
Bufflehead	F	R	a	-	C	F
Common Goldeneye	C	O	a	a	C	C
Barrow's Goldeneye	a	-	-	-	-	a
Hooded Merganser *	U	U	R	R	F	R
Red-breasted Merganser °	C	F	O	O	C	F
Common Merganser	F	R	O	O	F	F
Ruddy Duck *	C	U	R	R	F	R
Osprey °	O	R	O	R	U	-
Bald Eagle	R	O	a	O	R	R
Northern Harrier *	U	R	U	F	R	
Sharp-shinned Hawk °	R	R	O	F	F	O
Cooper's Hawk *	R	U	U	U	U	R
Northern Goshawk	a	a	-	a	O	O
Red-shouldered Hawk *	R	R	R	R	R	R
Broad-winged Hawk *	R	F	R	F	R	a
Swainson's Hawk * (l)	O	O	O	O	a	-
Red-tailed Hawk *	F	F	F	F	C	F
Rough-legged Hawk	U	R	a	a	U	U
Golden Eagle	a	a	a	a	O	a
American Kestrel *	U	U	U	U	U	U
Merlin	O	a	a	R	U	a
Peregrine Falcon *	R	R	R	U	U	R
Gray Partridge * (l)	O	O	O	O	O	O
Ring-necked Pheasant *	U	U	U	U	U	U
Wild Turkey (l)	O	O	O	O	O	O
Northern Bobwhite * (l)	R	R	R	R	R	
Yellow Rail	a	a	-	a	a	-
Black Rail	a	a	a	-	-	-
King Rail °	-	O	O	O	-	-
Virginia Rail *	O	U	U	U	O	O
Sora *	R	F	F	F	R	a
Common Moorhen *	a	U	U	U	a	a
American Coot *	C	C	U	C	C	R
Sandhill Crane	C	R	R	C	O	
Black-bellied Plover	-	U	F	F	U	a
American Golden-Plover	F	R	O	U	U	-
Semipalmated Plover	a	R	F	F	O	a
Piping Plover	a	O	O	O	a	-
Killdeer *	C	C	C	C	U	O
American Avocet	a	O	O	O	O	-
Greater Yellowlegs	U	U	U	U	U	-
Lesser Yellowlegs	U	F	C	C	U	-
Solitary Sandpiper	O	U	U	U	R	-
Willet	a	R	R	R	-	-
Spotted Sandpiper *	O	F	F	F	R	-
Upland Sandpiper * (l)	O	R	R	R	-	-

	ES	LS	Su	EF	LF	Wi
Whimbrel	-	R	O	R	-	-
Hudsonian Godwit	-	a	a	a	a	-
Marbled Godwit	-	O	O	O	a	-
Ruddy Turnstone	-	U	U	U	R	a
Red Knot	-	R	O	R	O	a
Sanderling	-	U	U	F	F	a
Semipalmated Sandpiper	a	U	C	C	U	-
Western Sandpiper	-	O	R	R	a	-
Least Sandpiper	R	U	C	C	O	a
White-rumped Sandpiper	-	U	a	R	O	-
Baird's Sandpiper	a	O	R	U	R	-
Pectoral Sandpiper	U	F	F	F	U	a
Purple Sandpiper	a	a	a	-	O	O
Dunlin	a	U	a	F	F	a
Stilt Sandpiper	-	R	U	U	-	-
Buff-breasted Sandpiper	-	-	R	R	O	-
Ruff/Reeve	a	a	a	a	-	-
Short-billed Dowitcher	a	U	F	F	R	-
Long-billed Dowitcher	-	a	O	O	R	-
Common Snipe °	U	R	R	F	U	O
American Woodcock *	U	U	U	U	R	a
Wilson's Phalarope	-	R	R	R	a	-
Red-necked Phalarope	-	a	a	a	a	-
Red Phalarope	-	-	a	a	O	a
Pomarine Jaeger	-	-	a	a	a	a
Parasitic Jaeger	-	-	-	R	R	a
Long-tailed Jaeger	-	-	a	a	a	-
Laughing Gull	a	O	O	O	O	-
Franklin's Gull	a	O	O	R	U	a
Little Gull	a	a	a	a	O	O
Black-headed Gull	a	a	a	a	-	-
Bonaparte's Gull	C	C	O	U	C	R
Mew Gull	a	-	-	-	a	O
Ring-billed Gull *	C	C	C	A	A	C
California Gull	a	-	-	a	a	a
Herring Gull *	C	C	F	C	C	C
Thayer's Gull	R	O	a	a	R	U
Iceland Gull	O	O	a	-	O	O
Lesser Black-backed Gull	O	O	a	a	O	O
Glaucous Gull	U	O	a	a	R	U
Great Black-backed Gull	R	O	a	a	O	R
Black-legged Kittiwake	a	a	-	a	R	O
Sabine's Gull	-	-	-	a	O	-
Caspian Tern °	R	U	U	F	R	-
Common Tern °	O	F	R	F	R	-
Forster's Tern °	R	U	R	F	R	-
Least Tern	-	a	a	-	-	-
Black Tern *	a	U	U	U	a	-
Rock Dove *	A	A	A	A	A	A
Mourning Dove *	F	C	C	A	C	F
Monk Parakeet * (l)	R	R	R	R	R	R
Black-billed Cuckoo *	-	U	U	R	a	-
Yellow-billed Cuckoo *	-	U	U	U	a	-
Barn Owl	a	a	-	a	a	a
Eastern Screech-Owl *	U	U	U	U	U	F
Great Horned Owl *	U	U	U	U	U	U
Snowy Owl (v)	a	-	-	-	O	R
Barred Owl * (l)	R	R	R	R	R	R
Long-eared Owl ° (v)	O	a	a	-	O	R

	ES	LS	Su	EF	LF	Wi
Short-eared Owl	U	R	a	a	U	U
Northern Saw-whet Owl	O	a	a	a	O	O
Common Nighthawk *	-	U	F	A	a	-
Chuck-will's-widow ° (l)	-	O	O	-	-	-
Whip-poor-will * (l)	O	U	U	O	a	-
Chimney Swift *	O	C	C	A	U	-
Ruby-throated Hummingbird *	O	U	U	U	O	-
Belted Kingfisher *	U	U	U	U	U	R
Red-headed Woodpecker *	U	F	F	F	U	R
Red-bellied Woodpecker *	F	F	F	F	F	F
Yellow-bellied Sapsucker	U	R	a	U	F	O
Downy Woodpecker *	F	F	F	F	F	F
Hairy Woodpecker *	U	U	U	U	U	U
Northern Flicker *	F	C	F	C	F	R
Pileated Woodpecker °	O	O	O	O	O	O
Olive-sided Flycatcher	-	R	O	R	a	-
Eastern Wood-Pewee *	-	C	C	F	a	-
Yellow-bellied Flycatcher	-	U	O	R	-	-
Acadian Flycatcher *	-	U	U	?	-	-
Alder Flycatcher *	-	U	U	?	-	-
Willow Flycatcher *	-	F	F	?	-	-
Least Flycatcher °	a	C	U	?	-	-
Eastern Phoebe *	F	U	U	F	O	-
Great Crested Flycatcher *	-	F	F	U	a	-
Western Kingbird °	-	a	a	a	a	-
Eastern Kingbird *	-	C	C	U	-	a
Northern Shrike	O	a	-	-	O	O
Loggerhead Shrike ° (l)	O	O	O	O	-	-
White-eyed Vireo * (l)	a	R	R	O	a	a
Bell's Vireo * (l)	-	R	R	O	a	-
Blue-headed Vireo	a	R	a	R	-	-
Yellow-throated Vireo *	-	U	U	R	a	-
Warbling Vireo *	-	C	C	F	a	-
Philadelphia Vireo	-	U	a	U	O	-
Red-eyed Vireo *	a	C	C	F	O	-
Blue Jay *	F	C	F	F	F	F
American Crow *	A	A	A	A	A	A
Horned Lark *	F	F	U	U	F	F
Purple Martin *	R	F	F	C	a	-
Tree Swallow *	F	F	F	F	R	a
Northern Rough-winged Swallow *	O	F	U	R	-	-
Bank Swallow *	O	F	U	R	a	-
Barn Swallow *	U	C	C	C	R	-
Cliff Swallow *	a	U	U	U	-	a
Black-capped Chickadee *	C	C	C	C	C	C
Tufted Titmouse * (l)	U	U	U	U	U	U
Red-breasted Nuthatch ° (v)	U	R	a	U	F	R
White-breasted Nuthatch *	F	F	F	F	F	F
Brown Creeper °	F	R	a	U	F	R

	ES	LS	Su	EF	LF	Wi
❑ Carolina Wren * (l)	R	R	R	R	R	R
❑ House Wren *	a	C	C	U	a	a
❑ Winter Wren	U	R	a	R	F	O
❑ Sedge Wren *	O	U	U	R	O	-
❑ Marsh Wren *	R	F	F	U	R	a
❑ Golden-crowned Kinglet °	F	O	a	O	F	R
❑ Ruby-crowned Kinglet	U	F	-	U	F	a
❑ Blue-gray Gnatcatcher *	R	U	U	R	-	-
❑ Eastern Bluebird *	U	U	U	U	U	O
❑ Veery *	O	F	U	U	O	-
❑ Gray-cheeked Thrush	a	U	a	U	O	a
❑ Swainson's Thrush	a	C	a	C	O	a
❑ Hermit Thrush	F	F	a	F	F	R
❑ Wood Thrush *	a	F	F	U	a	-
❑ American Robin *	C	A	A	A	C	U
❑ Varied Thrush	a	a	-	-	a	a
❑ European Starling *	A	A	A	A	A	A
❑ Gray Catbird *	a	C	C	C	U	a
❑ Northern Mockingbird * (l)	O	R	O	a	a	a
❑ Brown Thrasher *	R	F	F	U	R	a
❑ American Pipit	O	R	-	O	R	-
❑ Bohemian Waxwing	a	a	-	-	a	a
❑ Cedar Waxwing *	F	F	F	C	F	F
❑ Blue-winged Warbler *	a	F	F	U	-	-
❑ Golden-winged Warbler *	-	U	R	U	-	-
❑ Tennessee Warbler	a	C	O	C	O	-
❑ Orange-crowned Warbler	O	U	a	R	R	a
❑ Nashville Warbler	O	C	a	C	R	a
❑ Northern Parula *	a	U	a	R	a	-
❑ Yellow Warbler *	a	C	C	F	O	a
❑ Chestnut-sided Warbler °	a	C	R	F	O	-
❑ Magnolia Warbler	O	C	a	C	R	a
❑ Cape May Warbler	-	U	a	U	O	a
❑ Black-throated Blue Warbler	-	R	a	R	a	-
❑ Yellow-rumped Warbler	U	A	a	C	C	R
❑ Black-throated Green Warbler °	a	C	O	C	R	-
❑ Blackburnian Warbler	-	U	O	U	a	-
❑ Yellow-throated Warbler °	a	O	a	-	-	a
❑ Pine Warbler	O	R	-	R	O	a
❑ Prairie Warbler ° (l)	a	R	R	R	-	-
❑ Palm Warbler	O	C	a	C	F	a
❑ Bay-breasted Warbler	a	C	a	C	R	-
❑ Blackpoll Warbler	a	C	a	C	O	-
❑ Cerulean Warbler * (l)	-	U	U	O	a	-
❑ Black-and-white Warbler °	O	F	O	F	R	-
❑ American Redstart *	a	C	U	C	U	a
❑ Prothonotary Warbler * (l)	a	R	R	R	-	a
❑ Worm-eating Warbler	a	O	a	a	-	-
❑ Ovenbird *	a	F	U	U	O	a
❑ Northern Waterthrush	a	F	a	F	R	a
❑ Louisiana Waterthrush *	R	R	R	O	-	a
❑ Kentucky Warbler * (l)	a	O	O	a	-	-
❑ Connecticut Warbler	-	R	a	R	a	-
❑ Mourning Warbler °	-	U	R	R	a	-
❑ Common Yellowthroat *	O	C	C	F	R	a
❑ Hooded Warbler * (l)	a	R	R	O	a	-
❑ Wilson's Warbler	-	F	a	F	a	a
❑ Canada Warbler °	-	U	O	R	-	-
❑ Yellow-breasted Chat *	-	U	U	O	-	a
❑ Summer Tanager °	a	O	O	-	-	-
❑ Scarlet Tanager *	-	F	F	R	a	-
❑ Western Tanager	-	a	-	-	-	-
❑ Eastern Towhee *	U	F	F	U	R	O
❑ Spotted Towhee	-	a	-	-	a	a
❑ American Tree Sparrow	C	R	-	a	F	C
❑ Chipping Sparrow *	R	F	F	F	U	a
❑ Clay-colored Sparrow °	a	R	a	R	O	a
❑ Field Sparrow *	R	C	C	F	F	R
❑ Vesper Sparrow *	R	U	U	U	R	a
❑ Lark Sparrow * (l)	a	R	R	O	a	-
❑ Lark Bunting	a	a	-	a	-	a
❑ Savannah Sparrow *	F	C	C	F	U	a
❑ Grasshopper Sparrow *	a	U	U	R	a	-
❑ Henslow's Sparrow * (l)	a	R	R	O	a	-
❑ Le Conte's Sparrow	O	R	-	R	R	a
❑ Nelson's Sharp-tailed Sparrow	a	R	-	R	R	-
❑ Fox Sparrow	F	R	-	O	U	R
❑ Song Sparrow *	C	C	C	C	C	F
❑ Lincoln's Sparrow	O	U	a	U	U	a
❑ Swamp Sparrow *	U	F	U	F	F	R
❑ White-throated Sparrow	U	C	O	C	C	U
❑ Harris's Sparrow	a	O	a	a	O	a
❑ White-crowned Sparrow	O	F	a	R	F	R
❑ Dark-eyed Junco	C	R	a	U	A	A
❑ Lapland Longspur	U	O	-	a	U	U
❑ Smith's Longspur (l)	O	-	-	a	a	-
❑ Snow Bunting	U	a	-	-	U	F
❑ Northern Cardinal *	A	A	A	A	A	A
❑ Rose-breasted Grosbeak *	a	F	F	F	R	a
❑ Blue Grosbeak * (l)	-	O	O	-	-	-
❑ Indigo Bunting *	a	C	C	R	a	a
❑ Dickcissel *	-	U	U	O	a	a
❑ Bobolink *	-	F	F	U	a	-
❑ Red-winged Blackbird *	C	A	A	A	A	R
❑ Eastern Meadowlark *	U	F	F	U	F	R
❑ Western Meadowlark *	R	R	R	R	R	a
❑ Yellow-headed Blackbird *	R	U	U	R	a	a
❑ Rusty Blackbird	U	R	-	R	F	O
❑ Brewer's Blackbird °	O	O	O	O	O	a
❑ Common Grackle *	A	A	A	A	A	R
❑ Brown-headed Cowbird *	F	C	C	U	C	R
❑ Baltimore Oriole *	a	F	F	U	O	a
❑ Orchard Oriole * (l)	-	U	U	O	-	-
❑ Pine Grosbeak (v)	a	-	-	a	a	a
❑ Purple Finch	U	U	a	R	U	U
❑ House Finch *	C	C	C	C	C	F
❑ Red Crossbill ° (v)	U	a	a	a	U	U
❑ White-winged Crossbill (v)	O	a	-	-	a	O
❑ Common Redpoll (v)	R	a	-	-	R	U
❑ Hoary Redpoll	a	-	-	a	a	a
❑ Pine Siskin °	U	R	a	a	U	U
❑ American Goldfinch *	F	F	C	C	C	F
❑ Evening Grosbeak (v)	R	a	-	a	R	R
❑ House Sparrow *	A	A	A	A	A	A

Index of Scientific Names

This index references only the primary, illustrated species descriptions.

Index of Common Names

Numbers in boldface type refer to illustrated species descriptions.

About the Authors

When he's not out watching birds, frogs or snakes, Chris Fisher researches endangered species management and wildlife interpretation at the University of Alberta in Edmonton. The appeal of wildlife and wilderness has led him on many travels, including frequent visits with birds, throughout North America and as far away as Thailand. By sharing his enthusiasm and passion for wild things through lectures, photographs and articles, Chris strives to foster a greater appreciation for the value of our wilderness.

David Johnson brings to this project more than 25 years of birding experience in the Chicago area. He is an avid birder, tour leader and writer, and he is currently an associate editor of the *Meadowlark*, a journal of Illinois birds published by the Illinois Ornithological Society. David is heavily involved in the local birding community, leading field trips and organizing and participating in many breeding bird surveys and Christmas and spring bird counts. He is a member of nine local, regional and national birding associations. In 1996, the Chicago Audubon Society named David a Protector of the Environment, and in 1998 it awarded him a Silver Anniversary honor for long-term service to the birds and birders of Chicagoland.